# Moorish Fusion Cuisine
## Conquering the New World

## Zouhair Zairi

# Moorish Fusion Cuisine
## Conquering the New World

## Zouhair Zairi

EMERALD
BOOK CO.

To my wonderful wife, Yuka, and my two boys, Noah and Taha, who are my source of unending support and joy. And to my mother and my father.

— *Chef* Zouhair Zairi

To you, the reader, it is my honor and privilege to invite you to have a Moorish fusion meal filled with flavors.

— *Chef* Zouhair Zairi

# Contents

# Foreword

By reading this book you will discover the passion that Zouhair Zairi has for his Moroccan roots. There is nothing as noble as carrying on the old traditions of an ethnic culture and blending them with modern ways. You will find that these recipes reflect Zouhair's outgoing personality. He creates modern Moorish cuisine without sacrificing the traditional flavors, while also retaining basic cooking techniques. I have known Zouhair, "Zack," for the last twenty years. He is not only a great chef, but he is also a great friend and family man. His dedication to his work is unique, and I was proud to have him by my side in various kitchens.

**Christian Chemin**
*Executive Chef*
Maître Cuisinier de France
Member, l'Academie Culinaire de France

**Christian Chemin**
*Executive Chef*
Maître Cuisinier de France

# Introduction

I'm proud to say that I'm a descendant of the early Moors, who were of mixed Arabic and Berber heritage. My ancestors were intellectually curious, religiously tolerant, and highly educated. When the Moors sailed from Morocco in northwest Africa and conquered Spain in 711 AD, they heralded an enlightened age at a time when the rest of Europe remained in the dark. For the next seven hundred years, *Al-Andalus*, as the Iberian Peninsula was called in Arabic, would flourish. The Moors were extremely advanced in astronomy, mathematics, architecture, and philosophy, and they promoted education for all. Beautiful cities, like Granada, Córdoba, and Seville, boasted waterways, sewer systems, streetlights, and exquisite architectural marvels. The finest example of Moorish architecture, the Alhambra palace in Granada, was built in accordance with advanced geometric principles.

The Moors' agricultural skills were put to use in the cultivation of olives, almonds, saffron, grapes, pomegranates, artichokes, and palms. Their cuisine incorporated cinnamon, chilies, and other spices traded from as far as China and from other areas that had been visited or conquered by Arabian forces. Their diet could be described as Mediterranean, containing an abundance of ingredients from their region: fish, shellfish, citrus fruits, aromatic essences, and flowers. The Moorish people created amazing cuisine, which still inspires chefs and diners to this day.

Iberia's era of Islamic rule ended in 1492, when Catholics took over Granada and began to eradicate all memories of the existence of Muslims (as well as Jews and other non-Christians). As Ferdinand and Isabella sent Christopher Columbus to expand their power, my Berber ancestors retreated to Morocco, where the population continued to uphold the high standards set by those early Moorish conquerors.

My own family was well educated. I was expected to become an engineer, but I'd wanted to come to America since I was a young boy. I fantasized about cowboys and Indians and believed that success of every kind was possible there, if you worked hard. I dreamt of conquering the New World.

Although he had no confidence in me when I was nineteen, my father nevertheless gave me permission to go abroad and try my luck in the United States. I crossed the Atlantic with little money but big dreams.

I fell into the restaurant business almost immediately, and for the many years that followed I learned everything from the ground up. I worked hard, sometimes too hard. I tell people that I graduated from the "school of hard knocks." I became skilled in classic French cuisine, but I soon realized that it would take more than that to become a good chef. I've since learned that it takes unfailing dedication and uncompromising standards to use the best ingredients. It also involves a passion for food that keeps your creative ideas in overdrive, even when you've been standing on your feet for twelve hours a day, seven days straight.

Becoming a chef was my destiny. Looking back, I can now see that fate took me by the ear and granted me a wish I sent to the universe when I was just ten years old. A friend of the family worked in the prince's quarters of the king's palace in Rabat, Morocco. One day I was invited to spend an afternoon in my friend's company. As a treat, he brought me a piece of cake that had been baked in the royal kitchens. It was the most delicious pastry I've ever tasted, and I remember thinking, "When I grow older, I want to be able to make something this wonderful." I forgot all about that wish until well after I'd begun my culinary career.

Living in the United States, I experimented with my own versions of Morocco's Berber cuisine, drawing on fond memories of my mother's and grandmother's cooking and our many trips to the farmers' markets. My grandmother was an excellent chef, a natural, you might say. I loved hanging out in her kitchen, grinding almonds for her pastries and rolling the dough for her savory flat breads.

Over time, the delicious dishes I grew up with were fused with influences from the many regions of America where I'd lived and worked. Southern, northwestern, western, and island styles of cooking naturally melded with Moorish cuisine in my mind's eye—the place from which I begin to create.

My approach is to showcase the ingredients and keep it simple. I have a knack of combining herbs and spices and transforming them into complex, aromatic blends that I sprinkle onto meat, poultry, and fish. I enjoy using traditional ingredients, like rose petals, orange blossom water, and precious argan oil, in new ways. I add rose water to my vinaigrettes, which adds a beautiful fragrance and is soothing to the palate. The colors and textures of food are sexy to me, and I'm aware of how food is important for good health. I often remember an old Chinese proverb: "When you think of good food, you think of good health." You'll find olive oil in all of my dishes, as it's an integral part of a Mediterranean diet and it helps sustain a long life. I also enjoy working with contrasts, like fire and ice, as in my Hamachi Crudo. You bite into the cold, fresh fish and suddenly there's a little kick from a dot of Harissa. My cuisine engages all five senses. We eat first with the eyes, so food must be visually appealing, and presentation itself is an art form.

I believe that a chef is only as good as his or her ingredients. I use organic products and local produce, free-range game, poultry, eggs, and meat. My motto is "Fresh, fresh, fresh!"

This cookbook has been compiled by a Moroccan-born chef. It represents authentic Moorish cuisine fused with new elements, artfully combined to create fresh tastes for your enjoyment. It pays homage to the skill of all the Moroccan chefs, the majority of whom are women. It's my heart and soul food.

Bon appétit!
Chef ZZ
**Zouhair Zairi**

# About the Chef

Feeling restless and eager to follow his dream of becoming a success in America, Zouhair Zairi left his family in Morocco and touched down in New York at the tender age of nineteen. He'd become an immigrant overnight, with five hundred dollars in his pocket and no plan in mind.

His first job was washing dishes in a Mediterranean restaurant in Atlanta. After a while his responsibilities were increased and he was encouraged to learn all aspects of the business. His next career move took him to a restaurant/bakery, where he learned how to roll pastry, organize schedules, and sort out the payroll. Zouhair flourished as a team player. His skill in money management and his artist's eye for food presentation led him to a rewarding career in the hospitality/culinary industry. His gastronomic abilities include casual to fine dining, planning and execution of large banquets, and cooking Southern food.

For two decades he worked on both sides of the house. He earned an associate's degree in hospitality management, made the Dean's list at Gwinnett College in Atlanta, and gained a scholarship from the American Hotel & Lodging Educational Foundation. As an exceptionally gifted executive banquet chef, he created intricate food presentations for the 1996 Olympic tennis team's "Gala Affair."

During his years with the Capital City Country Club in Atlanta, he was recognized as Manager of the Month and in 1999, he was named Employee of the Year. Training in classic cuisine, Zouhair advanced to become an executive sous chef, mentored by esteemed Master Chef of France Christian Chemin. With Christian's guidance he planned and hosted the nineteenth Master Chefs of France elite dinner.

In 2002 Zouhair became the executive chef and director of his own restaurant, Spices. It was named Best New Restaurant in Maui by *Maui No Ka 'Oi Magazine*. While there, he enjoyed cooking many succulent plates, including his signature dishes, Seafood Salad and Roasted Beets Salad with Vanilla Bean Oil. Two years later he moved on from Spices to work at a five-diamond resort. His abilities and passion earned him the coveted Culinary Excellence Award from the JW Marriott Resort & Spa and a Certificate of Appreciation from the White House.

Now, at the age of forty, "ZZ" has come full circle. Having accomplished his dream of becoming a success in the culinary world, his greatest joy is spending time at home with his wife and two sons, Taha, three, and Noah, eight. He reports that his new "occupation" is developing his softer side and cultivating a deep admiration for a mother's flexibility and strength.

Along with providing consulting services to other restauranteurs, inspired by his Berber heritage, Zouhair moonlights (literally) in the wee hours of the morning. He can often be found in his restaurant-style home kitchen creating new recipes for his first cookbook, *Moorish Fusion Cuisine: Conquering the New World*.

# Soups

# Golden Gazpacho

This is a perfect starter if you want to impress guests on a hot summer day. We are so fortunate to have access to all kinds of different colorful produce. In this recipe we substitute yellow tomatoes and yellow peppers without sacrificing the taste of traditional gazpacho. Using lump crabmeat as a garnish adds a nice finish to this elegant chilled soup.

2 pounds yellow tomatoes, peeled and grated
1 European cucumber, peeled, seeded, and chopped
2 yellow peppers, cored, seeded, and chopped
1 small Vidalia onion, chopped
2 garlic cloves, minced
3 tablespoons cider vinegar
½ cup extra-virgin olive oil
1 to 2 cups water (if needed)
Kosher salt to taste
Ground white pepper to taste

**Garnish:**
Extra-virgin olive oil
Cider vinegar
2 ounces lump crabmeat
Fresh cilantro

**Preparation:** 20 minutes

Serves 4 to 6

**Method:**

Put the yellow tomatoes, cucumber, yellow peppers, onion, garlic, and vinegar in a blender; process until smooth. While the blender is still running, add the oil slowly, in a thin stream. If the mixture is too thick, add a little water as needed for the desired consistency. Season with salt and pepper and refrigerate overnight.

Before serving, taste and adjust seasoning, then strain.

To serve, pour the gazpacho into medium soup bowls and drizzle each serving with a little extra-virgin olive oil and cider vinegar. Top with lump crabmeat and a few cilantro leaves. Serve at once.

# Traditional Andalusia Gazpacho

Gazpacho originated in Andalusia, an autonomous region of Spain located on the southern tip of the Iberian peninsula. The country's name derives from the Arabic *Al-Andalus*, the name given to Spain under Muslim rule between the eigth and fifteenth centuries.

5 ripe tomatoes, peeled and
 chopped
1 European cucumber, peeled,
 seeded, and coarsely chopped
1 green bell pepper, coarsely
 chopped
1 Vidalia onion, coarsely
 chopped
2 garlic cloves, minced
3 tablespoons sherry vinegar
½ cup extra-virgin olive oil
Kosher salt to taste
Freshly ground black pepper
 to taste

**Garnish:**

Croutons
2 cherry tomatoes, cut in
 quarters
Extra-virgin olive oil
1 tablespoon chives

**Preparation:** 20 minutes

Serves 4 to 6

**Method:**

Put the tomatoes, cucumber, green pepper, onion, garlic, and vinegar in a blender and process until the mixture is smooth. While the blender is still running, add the oil in a thin stream until the mixture is as smooth as possible. Season with salt and pepper.

Strain through a food mill, pressing all the solids with the back of a ladle. Refrigerate overnight. The longer the gazpacho sits, the more all the flavors will develop.

Taste and adjust seasoning if needed.

To serve, pour the gazpacho into small soup bowls. Place a few croutons and 2 cherry tomato quarters on top of each serving. Drizzle with extra-virgin olive oil, sprinkle with chives, and serve at once.

# White Gazpacho

This traditional white gazpacho is a legacy of the Moors. Most likely it originated when the Moors ruled Andalusia for almost eight centuries. In this version, I substitute a golden raisin garnish for the traditional green grape garnish.

4 slices day-old bread,
  crust removed
3 cups almond milk
  (reserve 1 cup)
2 cups blanched almonds
2 tablespoons garlic cloves
½ cup extra-virgin olive oil
½ cup sherry vinegar
Kosher salt to taste

**Garnish:**
Sherry Vinegar
¼ cup toasted sliced almonds
2 tablespoons golden raisins
Extra-virgin olive oil

**Preparation:** 40 minutes

Serves 4

**Method:**

Soak the day-old bread in almond milk for 15 to 20 minutes. In a food processor, blend the almonds and garlic until the mixture is smooth. Squeeze the almond milk from the soaked bread and reserve the liquid. Add the soaked bread, olive oil, and vinegar to the almond and garlic mix and blend until a smooth paste is formed. Add the remaining almond milk and blend until it reaches the desired consistency. Season with salt and chill overnight.

Before serving, season with a bit more Sherry vinegar. Ladle into small soup bowls. Garnish with almonds and golden raisins and drizzle with extra-virgin olive oil. Serve at once.

# Harira with Hard-Boiled Eggs and Dates

This a traditional Moroccan soup served in every household during the holy month of Ramadan, the month of fasting, and on cold winter days. There are many versions of this soup, depending on the region in Morocco. In this recipe based on my childhood memories, I try to simplify the preparation without sacrificing the taste.

1 pound lamb shoulder, trimmed and cut into small cubes

1 Vidalia onion, diced

½ cup celery with leaves, diced

2 teaspoons ground turmeric

1 teaspoon ground cinnamon

2 tablespoons smen (aged butter) (see Glossary)

2 (14-ounce) cans organic diced tomatoes

½ bunch cilantro

Pinch of saffron, pulverized

2 quarts water

1 (25-ounce) can cooked chickpeas

Freshly ground black pepper to taste

Kosher salt to taste

1 cup all-purpose flour mixed with 1 cup water

**Garnish:**

Lemon wedges

Hard-boiled eggs, cut into quarters

Dates

Ground cumin

**Preparation:** 20 minutes

**Cooking:** 2 hours

Serves 10 to 12

**Method:**

In a large stockpot cook the lamb, onion, celery, turmeric, and cinnamon in the butter for 5 to 10 minutes over low heat, stirring occasionally, until the lamb and onion turn golden brown.

Puree the tomatoes and cilantro in a blender. Add the tomato mixture and saffron to the soup pot and continue cooking for 15 to 20 minutes. Add 2 quarts of water and cook for 1 hour over medium heat. Halfway through the cooking process, add chickpeas and black pepper.

A few minutes before serving, season the soup with salt and thicken with the flour slurry, also known in Morocco as *tedouira*. Cook for 10 more minutes, stirring often to avoid any lumps.

To serve, ladle the soup into medium soup bowls. Garnish with squeezed lemon wedges, hard-boiled egg quarters, dates, and a sprinkle of cumin.

**Note:** In some Moroccan regions, the *tedouira* used to thicken harira is made a day in advance.

# Chilled Pumpkin Soup with Fresh Nutmeg and Toasted Almonds

Although pumpkin is known as a winter vegetable, in this recipe pumpkin is the base of a delicious cold soup, Moorish style, garnished with fresh nutmeg and almonds.

1 Vidalia onion, coarsely chopped
1 Granny Smith apple, peeled and diced
2 tablespoons olive oil
1 red kuri pumpkin or kabocha squash, peeled, seeded, and cut into medium chunks
2 tablespoons brown sugar
Pinch of saffron
1 cinnamon stick
3 quarts vegetable broth (see Basics)
½ cup almond milk
Kosher salt to taste
Ground white pepper to taste

**Garnish:**
Toasted slivered almonds
Fresh nutmeg, grated

**Preparation:** 15 minutes

**Cooking:** 40 minutes

Serves 10 to 12

**Method:**

In large soup pot, sauté onion and apple in olive oil over medium heat; add pumpkin and brown sugar and cook for 5 more minutes.

Add saffron, cinnamon stick, and vegetable broth and cook for 20 to 25 minutes or until pumpkin is tender and starting to dissolve. Remove the cinnamon stick.

Use a blender or a hand power mixer to puree all ingredients until smooth. Add almond milk and simmer for 5 minutes, making sure the soup is simmering after adding the milk. Do not boil. Season to taste and chill overnight.

To serve, ladle the soup into medium bowls. Garnish with toasted almonds and freshly grated nutmeg.

# Tomato, Fennel, and Saffron Soup
# with Olive Oil–Poached Artichokes

In this recipe I combine two of my favorite ingredients, fennel and artichoke.
This light, healthy, saffron broth is a perfect soup any time of the year.

4 whole artichokes, cleaned and
  quartered (leave stem on for
  presentation)
1 cup olive oil, reserving
  1½ tablespoons
2 quarts fennel broth
  (see Basics)
1 pinch saffron, toasted
1 shallot, julienned
2 garlic cloves, sliced very thin
1 whole fennel, julienned
  (reserve top part for stock)
8 organic grape tomatoes or
  cherry tomatoes
Kosher salt to taste
Freshly ground black pepper
  to taste

**Garnish:**
Zest of 1 lemon
Fresh parsley leaves

**Preparation:** 25 minutes

**Cooking:** 1 hour, 30 minutes

Serves 6 to 8

**Method:**

Poach the artichokes as follows. In a small sauce pot, over medium heat, place the artichoke quarters in the olive oil and poach for about 15 to 20 minutes or until the artichokes are tender. Keep warm.

In a medium soup pot, bring the fennel broth to warm, add the toasted saffron, and simmer for 30 to 45 minutes, allowing the saffron to release all its flavors.

Meanwhile, in a separate soup pot, heat 1 tablespoon of olive oil over medium heat. Sweat the shallot and garlic for a few minutes, stirring occasionally to make sure the shallot and garlic don't burn. Add the julienned fennel and cook for a few more minutes. Pour the saffron broth into the mixture and cook for 15 more minutes.

In a small sauté pan, heat ½ tablespoon of oil over high heat and sauté the tomatoes for a few seconds or until their skins start to blister. Add to the soup and simmer for 5 minutes. Season with salt and pepper.

To serve, ladle the soup into medium bowls and top with artichoke quarters crisscross. Sprinkle with lemon zest and garnish with fresh parsley leaves. Serve at once.

# Chilled Red and Yellow Pepper Soup with Toasted Almonds

This a perfect first course on a hot summer day. The combination of both soups served in the same bowl makes for an elegant presentation.

**Red pepper soup:**

3 red bell peppers, roasted,
   peeled, seeded, and chopped
1 tablespoon olive oil
2 shallots, roughly chopped
2 garlic cloves
1 sprig fresh thyme
2 tablespoons tomato paste
2 tablespoons sherry vinegar
1½ quarts chicken broth
   (see Basics)
Kosher salt to taste
Freshly ground black pepper
   to taste

**Yellow pepper soup:**

3 yellow peppers, seeded and
   chopped
1 tablespoon olive oil
2 shallots, roughly chopped
2 garlic cloves
2 pinches saffron
2 tablespoons sherry vinegar
1½ quarts chicken broth
   (see Basics)
Kosher salt to taste
Freshly ground black pepper
   to taste

**Garnish:**

1 tablespoon slivered almonds,
   toasted

**Preparation:** 45 minutes

**Cooking:** 30 minutes

Serves 4 to 6

**Method:**

To make red pepper soup, preheat oven to 375°F. Roast the peppers for 45 minutes or until the skin turns charcoal black. Place the roasted peppers in a medium bowl, cover with plastic wrap, and let rest for about 10 minutes. This process allows the pepper to be peeled very easily. Peel peppers, seed, and chop.

Heat olive oil over medium heat in a small soup pot. Sauté shallots and garlic for a few minutes. Add the roasted peppers and thyme and cook for 10 minutes. Add tomato paste, sherry vinegar, and chicken broth and cook for 20 minutes. In a blender puree all ingredients until smooth. Strain through a medium strainer with the back of the ladle pressing on the solids to extract as much liquid as possible. Season with salt and pepper and chill overnight.

Make yellow pepper soup. Follow the recipe for red pepper soup above, but substitute roasted yellow peppers, add pinches of saffron instead of thyme, and omit tomato paste.

To serve, use two pitchers, one filled with chilled red pepper soup, the second with chilled yellow pepper soup, one in each hand. Pour the soup simultaneously into a medium bowl for a fancy presentation. Garnish with toasted almonds and serve at once.

# Seafood Soup with Hawaiian Spiny Lobster and Amlou Crostini

This soup is inspired by the harvest of seafood found in the Mediterranean Sea. Living on Maui, surrounded by pristine waters, brings out memories of growing up in the Mediterranean region. This luxury soup is fit for a king. You can substitute any seafood available in your area and any firm fish. This is a meal in itself.

8 large shrimp (size 13–15)

4 lobster tails, halved

3 tablespoons olive oil, divided

1 sliver orange zest

1 Vidalia onion, finely chopped

1 leek, white part only, julienned

3 garlic cloves, crushed

2 (14-ounce) cans organic diced tomatoes

1 fennel bulb, julienned

3 quarts lobster broth (see Basics)

¾ teaspoon paprika

Pinch of saffron, pulverized

2 red bell peppers, roasted, peeled, seeded, and julienned

1 pound fresh clams (soak in water)

2 tablespoons amlou (see Glossary)

Kosher salt to taste

Freshly ground black pepper to taste

**Garnish:**

½ bunch cilantro, chopped

½ bunch flat-leaf parsley, chopped

Italian parsley, chopped

Rustic bread, sliced

Amlou (see Glossary)

**Preparation:** 45 minutes

**Cooking:** 1 hour

Serves 6 to 8

**Method:**

In a small bowl, combine the shrimp, lobster tail halves, one tablespoon of olive oil, and orange zest. Mix well and refrigerate. In a large stockpot, warm 2 tablespoons of olive oil over medium heat. Sauté the onion until softened, add leek, garlic, and tomatoes and cook for 15 minutes. Add fennel, lobster broth, paprika, and saffron and continue cooking for 25 minutes.

Meanwhile, in a small pan, sauté the roasted peppers. Set aside and keep warm.

Ten minutes before the soup is finished, add clams to the stockpot. Cook for a couple of minutes or until the shells start to open up. Add the shrimp and lobster and simmer for a few more minutes.

In a small bowl, whisk 1 cup of soup broth with 2 tablespoons of amlou. Return the mixture to the soup; season with salt and pepper.

To serve, arrange roasted peppers in medium soup bowls. Ladle in a few clams (with shells) and place 2 shrimp in each bowl. Ladle in soup broth, top it with a half lobster tail, and sprinkle fresh cilantro and parsley on top. Serve with rustic bread spread with amlou.

# Appetizers, Mezze, and Tapas

# Mackerel Croquettes

These delectable croquettes are a recollection from my childhood in Morocco,
when my mother would make delicious sardine meatballs. In this recipe
I substitute mackerel for the sardines.

---

4 mackerel, cleaned, deboned,
  skinned, and chopped
$\frac{2}{3}$ cup grated manchego
  cheese
1 tablespoon fresh lemon juice
1 egg yolk
1 clove garlic, minced
½ teaspoon paprika
3 tablespoons cilantro, chopped
Kosher salt to taste
Freshly ground black pepper
  to taste
1 cup all-purpose flour
1 whole egg, beaten
1 cup bread crumbs
Vegetable oil for frying

**Garnish:**
Harissa (see Basics)
Lemon wedges

**Preparation:** 20 minutes

**Cooking:** 5 minutes

Serves 4

**Method:**

In a medium bowl, combine mackerel, manchego cheese, lemon juice, egg yolk, garlic, paprika, and cilantro. Mix well and season with salt and pepper. Set aside and chill for an hour to firm up.

Shape the croquettes in either of two ways: (1) Wet hands and roll mixture into 1½-inch meatballs; (2) use two teaspoons and create a quenelle (rough oval egg shape), and repeat for each croquette.

Dredge each croquette in flour, then in egg wash, and finally in bread crumbs. Heat vegetable oil in a 10-inch frying pan over medium heat. Fry the croquettes for about 4 to 5 minutes until golden brown. Drain on paper towels sprinkled with kosher salt. Serve with harissa and lemon wedges on the side.

# Heirloom Tomato Bruschetta with 50-Year-Old Balsamic Vinegar

The sweetness of heirloom tomatoes and the saltiness of anchovies make a great contrast. The use of 50-year-old balsamic vinegar takes this simple bruschetta to another level of sophistication.

1 baguette, cut into
¼-inch-thick slices
2 garlic cloves, halved
4 tablespoons extra-virgin
olive oil
1 pound baby heirloom
tomatoes, cut in chunks
2 to 3 leaves fresh basil, torn
into small pieces
Cracked black pepper to taste
12 oil-packed silver anchovies,
rinsed
3 tablespoons 50-year-old
balsamic vinegar

**Preparation:** 20 minutes

Serves 4

**Method:**

Toast baguette slices over a hot grill (or in a toaster oven) for a couple of minutes until crisp on both sides. Lightly rub one side with a garlic half and drizzle with extra-virgin olive oil. Top with tomatoes and season with basil and pepper. Lay the anchovies on top of the tomato bruschetta and drizzle with the vinegar. Serve at once.

# Sweet Prawns with Lemon Olive Oil

This recipe is inspired by one of my favorite foods, sushi. This succulent dish showcases the natural sweetness of raw shrimp, enhanced by lemon oil and complemented by the saltiness of salmon roe.

2 whole lemons

12 fresh sweet shrimp, whole

2 tablespoons fresh squeezed lemon juice

1 tablespoon lemon olive oil (see Basics)

4 ounces salmon roe

**Garnish:**

Microgreens (optional)

**Preparation:** 10 minutes

**Cooking:** 5 minutes

Serves 4

**Method:**

Wash lemons, wrap them in foil, and roast in a 350°F oven for about 30 minutes. Unwrap, slice into ½-inch chips, and sear.

To prepare the shrimp, remove the heads and set aside. Shell each prawn, leaving the tail on. Gently cut a slit down the back of each prawn and remove the dark vein from the back of each. Rinse lightly under cold water and pat dry.

Preheat oven to 375°F. Bake the shrimp heads for 5 to 10 minutes, or until they are red. Keep hot.

To serve, press 3 prawns out flat on a serving plate. Drizzle a little lemon juice and lemon olive oil on each shrimp. Top with salmon roe. On the same plate, place 2 roasted prawn heads on top of a lemon chip. Garnish with microgreens if desired. Serve at once.

# Hamachi Crudo with Apple-Cucumber Slaw

Hamachi, also known as yellowtail, is a common ingredient in Japanese sushi. A versatile fish, it can be broiled, baked, or grilled. In this recipe it is served as a light starter, crudo-style (raw) to showcase the hamachi's luxurious taste.

8 ounces fresh hamachi

4 tablespoons lemon olive oil
(see Basics)

2 tablespoons lemon zest

Kosher salt to taste

1 tablespoon harissa
(see Basics)

**Apple-cucumber slaw:**

1 Granny Smith apple, peeled, cored, and julienned

1 medium European cucumber, julienned

2 tablespoons grapeseed oil

½ teaspoon sugar

½ tablespoon white balsamic vinegar

Kosher salt to taste

Freshly ground black pepper to taste

**Preparation:** 20 minutes

Serves 2

**Method:**

Cut the hamachi against the grain into 3-inch-long by 2-inch-wide pieces.

For the slaw, toss apple, cucumber, grapeseed oil, sugar, and vinegar in a small bowl to combine. Season with salt and pepper. Set aside and chill.

To assemble, lay 3 slices of hamachi side by side on each serving plate. Drizzle with lemon olive oil and sprinkle lemon zest and salt on each slice. Spoon small amounts of apple-cucumber slaw in between the hamachi. Place a dab of harissa on each hamachi slice and serve at once.

# Fava Bean Dip with Cumin and Extra-Virgin Olive Oil

This dish is very popular among Berbers and lovers of olive oil. It is usually served in the consistency of soup, and called bissara. In this recipe it is prepared as a dip to be shared among friends and family as a starter before the main meal.

2 cups dried fava beans
1 whole onion
1 bay leaf
2 garlic cloves, minced
4 tablespoons extra-virgin olive
  oil
1 teaspoon ground cumin
Zest of 1 lemon
Kosher salt to taste
White pepper to taste

**Garnish:**
4 tablespoons extra-virgin
  olive oil
Paprika
Fresh parsley
4 flat breads (see page 70)

**Cooking:** 1 hour

Serves 8

**Method:**

Soak the fava beans overnight in a medium pot full of water. The next day, drain the beans and wash well.

In a medium pot filled with 2 quarts water, combine the beans, onion, and bay leaf, bring to a boil, and cook over medium heat for an hour or until the beans are soft. Drain the beans, discard the onion and bay leaf, and reserve 1 cup of cooking liquid.

In a blender, combine cooked beans (about 3 cups), garlic, olive oil, cumin, and lemon zest and puree until smooth. Add cooking liquid if necessary to thin the bean dip. Season with salt and pepper and keep warm.

To serve, place the dip in a bowl and drizzle olive oil on top. Sprinkle with a little paprika and chopped parsley. Serve with flat bread on the side.

# Anise Flat Bread with Smen (Aged Butter) and Fennel and Arugula Salad

Smen, which is preserved butter, is a popular ingredient among the Berber tribes in Morocco. When a Berber baby is born, the family makes a batch of butter and preserves it for years, to be used on the child's wedding day.

**Anise flat bread:**

¼ teaspoon dried yeast

½ cup lukewarm water

8 ounces all-purpose flour

1 tablespoon fennel seeds

¼ teaspoon sea salt

2 tablespoons olive oil, plus
   additional oil for frying

**Fennel and arugula salad:**

1 fennel bulb, thinly shaved

8 ounces arugula

1 red onion, julienned

2 tablespoons olive oil

Juice of 1 lemon

Kosher salt to taste

Freshly ground black pepper
   to taste

**Garnish:**

4 tablespoons smen
   (aged butter) (see Glossary)

1 tablespoon organic honey

**Preparation:** 30 minutes

**Cooking:** 5 to 10 minutes

Serves 4

**Method:**

Combine the yeast and water and set aside. In a medium bowl, mix the flour, fennel seeds, and sea salt. Check the yeast to make sure it is dissolved. Pour the yeast mixture slowly into the flour, incorporating it with your hands. Work out the lumps, kneading and slapping. When the flour and yeast mixture are completely combined, mix in the olive oil and keep kneading. Cover the dough and let it rest for 20 to 25 minutes.

Sprinkle a little flour on a work surface, turn out the dough, and cut it into 4 pieces. Heat a large cast-iron skillet over medium heat. Using a rolling pin, roll a piece of dough into a thin round. Rub a little oil on each side and place the round in the hot skillet. Cook until both sides have brown spots, about 2 minutes on each side. Remove and keep warm. Repeat the same process for the rest of the dough.

Make the fennel and arugula salad. In a medium bowl, toss together shaved fennel, arugula, onion, olive oil, and lemon juice. Season with salt and pepper, then chill in the refrigerator.

While the flat bread is still hot, spread a quarter of the smen on each piece. Top with a handful of fennel and arugula salad and drizzle with organic honey. Cut into quarters and serve at once.

# Bastilla Be Thon

Bastilla is traditionally made with squab or chicken. In recent years many nontraditional fillings have been used, such as shrimp and crabmeat. Here, I use tuna to make this savory appetizer. It is served with spicy harissa and a refreshing arugula salad to help cleanse the palate.

2 tablespoons olive oil
1 Maui or Vidalia onion, finely chopped
1 garlic clove, minced
1 teaspoon paprika
1 teaspoon ground cumin
8 ounces fresh tuna
1 tablespoon lemon zest
2 tablespoons cilantro, chopped
2 tablespoons parsley, chopped
Kosher salt to taste
Freshly ground black pepper to taste
8 sheets phyllo dough, thawed
½ cup unsalted butter, melted
4 tablespoons green olives, chopped
2 egg yolks

**Side salad:**
1 bunch arugula, washed
¼ Preserved lemon (see Basics)
1 shallot, julienned
1 tablespoon grapeseed oil
Freshly ground black pepper

**Garnish:**
Lemon wedges
Harissa (see Basics)

**Preparation:** 20 minutes

**Cooking:** 25 minutes

Serves 4 (Makes 2 5-inch bastilla)

**Method:**
In a medium skillet, heat olive oil over medium heat. Sauté the onion and garlic for 3 to 5 minutes, until the onion turns translucent. Add paprika, cumin, and tuna and cook for 4 to 5 minutes, until the fish begins to flake. Remove from heat and shred the tuna.

In a medium bowl, combine the tuna, onion, garlic, lemon zest, cilantro, and parsley. Season with salt and pepper and set aside to cool.

Place 4 stacked phyllo sheets on a cutting board. Cut them in half with a sharp knife. Brush the bottom of the 5-inch cast-iron skillet with melted butter. Arrange 4 half phyllo sheets on the bottom of the skillet, leaving a 1½-inch border of phyllo dough extending up the sides. Brush each one lightly with melted butter.

Spoon half the tuna mixture into the middle of each, sprinkle with olives, and place an egg yolk on top of the tuna filling, being careful not to break the egg yolk. Fold over the edges of the pastry to partially cover the filling. Place the remaining phyllo sheets on top of the filling and tuck them under the bottom to stay firm. Brush the remaining butter on top of the bastilla. Preheat the oven to 400°F. Bake the bastilla until golden brown, 20 to 25 minutes.

In a small bowl, combine arugula, preserved lemon, shallot, and grapeseed oil. Season with black pepper and chill.

Serve hot with the salad, lemon wedges, and harissa.

# Foie Gras of the Sea (Monkfish Liver) with Maui Onion and Date Jam, Toasted Country Bread

This recipe was created to pay tribute to Japanese chefs and their pioneer culinary work that has helped shape our tastebuds.

8 ounces monkfish liver (fresh)

1 tablespoon Maui Onion and Medjool Date Jam (see Basics)

Kosher salt

1 loaf country bread, sliced and toasted

Freshly ground black pepper

**Garnish:**

Pomegranate molasses

Extra-virgin olive oil

**Preparation:** 45 minutes

**Cooking:** 20 minutes

Serves 4

**Method:**

Using a small knife, remove blood vessels and any membrane from the fresh monkfish liver. Soak in salted water for about 15 minutes. Pat dry with a paper towel.

Place the monkfish liver on a piece of cheesecloth or plastic wrap. Roll the liver into a sausage-shaped cylinder about 2 inches in diameter. Next, tightly roll the liver in aluminum foil and seal the foil on both ends. Steam on a rack over boiling water for 20 minutes. Chill in the refrigerator until cold.

Unwrap the monkfish liver; the color should be orange-pink. Using a sharp knife, cut the liver into ½-inch slices.

To serve, arrange two slices of the poached monkfish liver on each plate and sprinkle with a pinch of cracked black pepper and kosher salt. Spoon 1 tablespoon of onion and date jam on each plate. Drizzle a little pomegranate molasses and olive oil around each plate. Serve with toasted country bread.

**Note:** If fresh monkfish liver is not available, substitute monkfish liver pâte (usually sold in an 8.5-ounce tube).

# Mussels (*Bouzroug*), Mother's Style

I believe my passion for cooking is hereditary, passed down to me from my grandmother and my mom. One of my mom's favorites dishes is *Bouzroug*. Here, I try to duplicate the same taste I remember eating during childhood and whenever I go back home to visit.

2 pounds fresh mussels
1 tablespoon extra-virgin
   olive oil
1 shallot, finely chopped
2 cloves garlic, minced
1 red pepper, roasted, cleaned,
   and diced
2 tablespoons tomato paste
1 teaspoon ground cumin
¼ preserved lemon, diced
   (see Basics)
Kosher salt to taste
Freshly ground black pepper
   to taste

**Garnish:**
1 loaf ciabatta bread, sliced on
   the diagonal
Fresh parsley, chopped
4 lemon wedges

**Preparation:** 20 minutes

**Cooking:** 30 minutes

Serves 4

**Method:**

Scrub the mussels under cold running water, discarding any broken ones, and cut off the beards. Place the mussels in a double boiler in batches, cover, and steam for 5 minutes or until the shells open up. Repeat the same process until all the mussels are done. Carefully remove the meat and set aside; discard the empty shells. Reserve 1 cup of the boiling liquid.

Heat olive oil in a medium saucepan. Add shallots and sauté for 2 minutes. Add garlic and roasted peppers and cook for 3 to 5 minutes more. Add tomato paste, the 1 cup of mussel liquid, and cumin and cook until almost dry. Add preserved lemon, season with salt and pepper, and simmer for 5 minutes. Add the mussels to the saucepan and cook over low heat until the mussels are heated through.

To serve, spoon the sauce into dishes. Top with a couple of slices of toasted ciabatta bread and 5 or 6 mussels; garnish with parsley. Serve hot with lemon wedges on the side.

# Marinated Moorish Olives

The Moors have been credited for their skills and techniques in agriculture, especially in the cultivation of olives. Thanks to the Moors' dynasty, Spain is the world's largest olive producer and olives are important ingredients in the Mediterranean diet. In this recipe I use Moroccan olives grown in the Atlas mountain region of Morocco, but you can substitute Spanish olives.

**Moroccan cured black olives:**

2 cups dry cured black olives

2 tablespoons harissa
  (see Basics)

1 tablespoon flat-leaf parsley,
  finely chopped

1 tablespoon extra-virgin
  olive oil

Freshly ground black pepper
  to taste

**Moroccan green olives:**

1 cup Moroccan green olives
  (rinsed in cold water)

1 tablespoon preserved lemon
  (see Basics)

2 tablespoons flat-leaf parsley,
  finely chopped

1 tablespoon extra-virgin
  olive oil

**Moroccan red olives:**

2 cups red olives (rinsed in cold
  water)

1 tablespoon preserved lemon
  (see Basics)

2 tablespoons harissa
  (see Basics)

1 tablespoon flat-leaf parsley,
  finely chopped

**Preparation:** 15 minutes

Serves 4 to 6

**Method:**

Prepare cured black olives as follows. In a medium bowl, mix all ingredients and chill overnight, allowing all the flavors to be released.

Prepare green olives and red olives in the same manner.

To serve, place all the marinated olives together in a serving dish, as an appetizer or alongside the main meal.

# Fresh Oysters with Preserved Lemon and Olive Relish

There are so many wonders in the oceans, and fresh oysters—believed to have aphrodisiac powers—rank at the top. The aromas of preserved lemon and olive relish complement the savory taste of raw oysters.

12 fresh oysters

**Preserved lemon and olive relish:**

1 shallot, finely chopped

1 cup Moroccan green olives, rinsed, pitted, and chopped

½ wedge preserved lemon, rinsed and chopped (see Basics)

Juice of ½ lemon

2 tablespoons olive oil

Freshly ground black pepper to taste

**Garnish:**

2 cups rock salt (for presentation)

1 tablespoon harissa (see Basics)

1 tablespoon chives, finely chopped

**Preparation:** 15 minutes

Serves 4

**Method:**

In a medium bowl, combine the shallot, olives, and preserved lemon. Toss with lemon juice and olive oil. Season with pepper and refrigerate.

Shuck the oysters and discard the empty half shells, leaving the oyster in the other half. Rinse with cold water.

Spread rock salt over a large platter. Arrange the oysters on top of the rock salt (the salt helps to steady the oysters). Spoon 1 teaspoon of olive relish onto each oyster, top each one with a tiny bit of harissa, sprinkle chives on top, and serve at once.

# Diver Scallops with Caramelized Shallots and Fennel Gratinée

The decadent taste of scallops is enhanced with a succulent mixture of caramelized shallots and organic fennel. Bread crumbs add a crunchy texture to the dish without overpowering the scallops.

4 tablespoons olive oil

1 large fennel bulb, cut in half

1 cup fennel broth (see Basics)

8 shallots, julienned

2 cloves garlic, minced

½ teaspoon paprika

½ teaspoon sugar

Kosher salt to taste

Freshly ground black pepper
  to taste

8 fresh diver scallops, shells on

1 cup bread crumbs

1 cup shredded manchego
  cheese

**Garnish:**

Fresh thyme sprigs

Fresh parsley sprigs

**Preparation:** 25 minutes

**Cooking:** 10 minutes

Serves 4

**Method:**

In a small sauté pan, heat 2 tablespoons of olive oil over medium heat. Sear the fennel bulb halves for a couple of minutes. Cover with fennel broth and cook for about 20 minutes or until the fennel becomes soft. Remove fennel and chop. (This step can be done ahead of time.)

In another sauté pan, heat the remaining 2 tablespoons of olive oil and sweat the shallots for 10 minutes. When they start turning brown, add garlic, paprika, and sugar and keep cooking until the shallots become shiny and fully caramelized. Remove from heat and fold in the chopped fennel. Season with salt and pepper and set aside.

Using a sharp paring knife, carefully open the scallop shells. Discard the empty half shells, leaving the scallop in the other half.

Arrange the scallops on the half shell on a flat sheet pan. Season each scallop with a pinch of kosher salt. Top each one with a small amount of the shallot-and-fennel mixture, then with bread crumbs and manchego cheese on top. Broil for 5 to 7 minutes or until lightly browned. Sprinkle with herbs and serve hot.

# Anchovy Dip

Also known as *bagna cauda* and originally from Piedmont, Italy, this wonderful dip is perfect to serve with crudités any time of the year. The first time I had this tasty dip was in Tokyo, where my sister-in-law served it to me on one of my visits.

½ cup olive oil
4 garlic cloves, minced
12 anchovies, drained and
   chopped
½ cup unsalted butter
Freshly ground pepper
1 tablespoon fresh parsley,
   chopped
1 loaf ciabatta bread
Harissa (see Basics)

**Vegetables for dipping:**
1 cucumber, cut into strips
8 cherry tomatoes
1 red bell pepper, cut into
   strips
4 radishes, cut in half
1 bunch green onion, cut
   against the bias using both
   white and green parts
8 asparagus spears

**Preparation:** 5 minutes

**Cooking:** 15 minutes

Serves 6 to 8

**Method:**

In a saucepan, heat the oil over medium heat. Sauté the garlic and anchovies until the anchovies dissolve. Stirring constantly, add the butter and mix. Season with pepper and garnish with parsley. Keep warm.

To serve, place the anchovy dip in a serving bowl or fondue pot. Place the raw vegetables on a platter to pass for dipping. Serve with ciabatta bread and harissa on the side.

**Note:** You can use any vegetables with this dip.

# Flat Bread with Caramelized Maui Onions, Cured Black Olives, and Manchego Cheese

The smell of fresh flat bread reminds me of my upbringing in Morocco, when each day my mom made flat bread served with extra-virgin olive oil and honey for a snack. This recipe is one of my versions of a flat-bread snack.

**Flat bread:**

¼ teaspoon dried yeast

½ cup lukewarm water

1 cup all-purpose flour

¼ teaspoon sea salt

2 tablespoons olive oil, plus
   additional oil for frying

**Caramelized Maui onions:**

4 tablespoons olive oil

2 Maui onions, julienned

1 red onion, julienned

2 garlic cloves, minced

1 teaspoon paprika

2 teaspoons granulated sugar

Kosher salt to taste

Freshly ground black pepper
   to taste

**Garnish:**

1 cup cured black olives, pitted
   and sliced

1½ cups shredded manchego
   cheese

1 tablespoon chopped parsley

**Preparation:** 45 minutes
**Cooking:** 5 to 10 minutes
Serves 4

**Method:**

Make flat bread as follows. Stir yeast into lukewarm water and set aside. In a medium bowl, mix the flour and salt using your hands. Check the yeast to make sure it is dissolved. Pour the water and yeast slowly into the flour, incorporating it with your hands. Work out the lumps, kneading and slapping. When completely combined, mix in the oil and keep kneading. Cover the dough and let it rest for 20 to 25 minutes.

Sprinkle a little flour on a work surface, turn out the dough, and cut it into 4 pieces. Heat a large cast-iron skillet over medium heat. Using a rolling pin, roll a piece of dough into a thin round. Rub a little oil on each side and place the round in the hot skillet. Cook until both sides have brown spots, about 2 minutes on each side. Remove and keep at room temperature. Repeat the same process for the rest of the dough.

Make the caramelized onions. In a large sauté pan, heat olive oil over medium heat. Add Maui onion and red onion and cook for about 10 minutes, or until they begin to turn light brown. Add garlic, paprika, and sugar and keep cooking until the onion mixture becomes shiny and caramelized. Season with salt and pepper. Keep warm.

To serve, place the flat bread on a baking sheet. Spread the bread with caramelized onions, using a quarter of the mixture on each flat bread. Top with cured black olives, and sprinkle manchego cheese on top. Bake at 375°F for 5 minutes or until the cheese melts. Sprinkle with parsley. Cut into quarters and serve hot.

# Deep-Fried Cauliflower with Saffron Batter

This dish brings back some wonderful memories of my mom's kitchen. Whenever I visit home, I crave certain foods. Deep-fried cauliflower is one of them. It is served as a side dish.

---

1 large cauliflower
1 cup all-purpose flour
1½ cups soda water
2 eggs
1 pinch saffron (pulverized)
Kosher salt to taste
Freshly ground black pepper
   to taste
Vegetable oil for frying

**Preparation:** 20 minutes

**Cooking:** 5 minutes

Serves 4

**Method:**

Clean and cut the cauliflower into medium florets, discarding the stalk and leaves. Steam for 10 to 15 minutes or until tender; do not overcook. Refrigerate.

Meanwhile, measure the flour into a medium bowl. Slowly add the soda water, mixing with a whisk to avoid any lumps. Add the eggs and saffron to the batter, season with salt and pepper, and let it rest for 5 to 10 minutes.

Heat the vegetable oil in a fryer to 350°F. Dip each cauliflower floret into the batter, then fry for 3 to 5 minutes, until golden. Remove from the oil with a slotted spoon and drain on a paper towel. Transfer to a serving dish and sprinkle salt on top. Serve hot.

# Clams and Moorish Sausage

Spicy lamb sausage (*merguez*) is a traditional North African food.
Combining clams creates a treat for all seafood and meat lovers.

2 pounds fresh clams
2 tablespoons extra-virgin
  olive oil
8 ounces *merguez* (see
  Glossary), sliced into rounds
2 shallots, chopped
2 garlic cloves, minced
1 tablespoon paprika
Fresh thyme (a few sprigs)
2 cups fennel broth (see
  Basics)
1 bay leaf
Kosher salt to taste
Freshly ground black pepper
  to taste

**Garnish:**

2 tablespoons chopped fresh
  parsley
4 lemon wedges
1 loaf ciabatta bread, sliced and
  toasted

**Preparation:** 10 minutes

**Cooking:** 20 minutes

Serves 4

**Method:**

Soak the clams in cold water for 30 minutes. Discard any broken clams or open ones. In a large sauté pan, heat 1 tablespoon of olive oil over medium heat, add the *merguez*, and cook for 3 to 5 minutes or until golden, stirring occasionally. Remove from heat and set aside. In the same sauté pan, heat 2 tablespoons of olive oil, stir in the shallots, garlic, paprika, and fresh thyme and cook for about 5 minutes. Add the fennel broth, bay leaf, salt, and pepper and bring to a boil. Add the clams, cover, and cook for 5 minutes. Add the cooked *merguez* at the last minute and simmer for a couple more minutes, until all the clams open up.

To serve, ladle the clams and sausage into medium deep dishes. Pour the broth over the clams and sausage and sprinkle with parsley. Serve hot, with lemon wedges and toasted bread on the side.

**Note:** You can substitute any spicy sausage available in your local grocery.

# Grilled Octopus with Paprika and Smoked Salt

Octopus is one of my favorite seafoods. It has a soft yet chewy texture. Although unfamiliar to many, it is very popular in the Mediterranean countries and in Japanese cuisine, and it can be served in many different ways. In this recipe, octopus is boiled and lightly grilled to bring out its sweetness, and is served with paprika and smoked salt.

2 pounds fresh octopus
2 tablespoons kosher salt
2 tablespoons sherry vinegar
Extra-virgin olive oil
1 tablespoon paprika
2 teaspoons smoked salt
Freshly ground black pepper
  to taste

**Garnish:**
1 lemon, cut into wedges

**Preparation:** 35 minutes

**Cooking:** 1 hour

Serves 6 to 8

**Method:**

Clean the octopus by removing eyes, beak, and ink sac (or ask your fishmonger to clean it). Wash very well under running cold water, making sure all the sand is removed from the suckers.

Bring a large pot of water to a boil. Add salt, vinegar, and octopus and cook for about 45 minutes to an hour. (It is very important to cook the octopus until tender. To test for tenderness, use kitchen shears to cut off a piece from the thick part of a tentacle and taste it.) Remove the octopus from the boiling water, or leave it to cool in the water to ensure the octopus will be very tender. Rub the octopus lightly with a clean towel to remove any loose skin.

Light a charcoal or gas grill or heat a barbecue hot plate to high heat. Cut the octopus into ¾-inch pieces using kitchen shears. Thread 3 to 5 pieces on metal skewers, brush lightly with olive oil, and grill for 3 to 5 minutes.

Serve the octopus hot off the grill. Place the octopus pieces on a serving platter, drizzle with a good amount of olive oil, and sprinkle paprika, smoked salt, and black pepper on top. Serve with lemon wedges on the side.

**Note:** Cooking a large octopus can take up to 2 hours.

# Hawaiian Salt-Cured Salmon with Fried Capers, Egg White, Salmon Roe, and Toast Points

Salted fish is a staple of the diet in Morocco. This recipe is
my version of gravlax, garnished with salmon caviar.

## Curing: Step 1

4 cups Hawaiian salt or kosher
   salt
3 cups granulated sugar
1 shallot, julienned
1 teaspoon white peppercorns
½ bunch fresh parsley, coarsely
   chopped
2 bay leaves, dry, coarsely
   chopped
1 salmon fillet (3 to 5 pounds,
   skin on, deboned)

## Marinating: Step 2

5 cups olive oil
½ bunch fresh dill
½ teaspoon white peppercorns

## Garnish:

1 egg white, grated
1 tablespoon capers, lightly
   fried
2 tablespoons salmon roe
Fresh dill
White bread, sliced, crust
   removed, toasted, and cut
   into points

**Preparation:** 15 minutes + 24 hours + 12 hours

Serves 8

## Method:

In a medium bowl, combine Hawaiian salt, sugar, shallots, 1 teaspoon of white peppercorns, parsley, and bay leaves; set aside. Lay the salmon fillet skin side down in a shallow dish; using tweezers, remove all the bones. Pat dry with a paper towel. Top the salmon fillet with the salt and sugar mixture, making sure the salmon is covered completely. Cover with parchment paper and plastic wrap. Place a heavy board on top and weigh it down with two heavy cans. Refrigerate for 24 hours.

After 24 hours, uncover the salmon and wash off the salt mixture with cold water. Pat dry with a paper towel. The salmon should be firm and the color a darker orange. Lay the salmon in a medium-deep dish. Pour the olive oil on top, making sure the salmon is fully covered with oil. Add the fresh dill and ½ teaspoon of white peppercorns. Refrigerate for at least 12 hours before serving.

To serve, slice the salmon lengthwise, toward the tail. Roll each salmon slice, then top it with egg white and a few fried capers. Garnish with salmon roe and a sprig of fresh dill. Roll a few more slices of salmon in the same manner and place on a serving platter. Serve at once, on toast points.

**Note:** Cured salmon can last for up to 7 days, as long as it is refrigerated and stored in olive oil.

# Scallops Crudo with Fennel Slaw and Sherry Vinegar Reduction

This is a perfect starter on a summer evening. The sweetness of the scallops combined with the sherry vinegar reduction makes a nice contrast, and the fennel slaw brings a refreshing finish to the palate.

2 cups sherry vinegar

½ cup organic honey

1 tablespoon lemon juice

1 tablespoon orange juice

½ teaspoon granulated sugar

1 tablespoon grapeseed oil

1 fennel bulb, thinly shaved

2 ounces radish sprouts

4 diver scallops (raw)

Kosher salt to taste

Freshly ground black pepper
  to taste

**Garnish:**

2 tablespoons extra-virgin
  olive oil

Fennel leaf

**Preparation:** 20 minutes

Serves 4

**Method:**

Place 2 cups of sherry vinegar in a small copper pot, and reduce to half over high heat. Add honey and reduce for 5 more minutes. Set aside and cool at room temperature.

In a medium bowl combine lemon juice, orange juice, sugar, and grapeseed oil to make a vinaigrette. In a separate bowl, combine fennel and sprouts and toss with the vinaigrette. Season with salt and pepper.

Cut each scallop into 3 thin slices. Spoon the fennel slaw onto a serving plate, top with sliced scallops, and drizzle with the sherry vinegar reduction. Drizzle with extra-virgin olive oil and garnish with fennel leaf. Serve chilled.

# Royalty Eggs with Gold Leaves

All over North Africa and across the Mediterranean, eggs are enjoyed as a snack or an appetizer, either hard-boiled, dipped in salt and cumin, or softly scrambled. In this recipe, I take it to the next level, in both taste and presentation. If you want to feel like royalty for a day and impress your guests, one evening try this unique approach to scrambled eggs.

8 organic large eggs (reserve
   4 shells for presentation)
¼ teaspoon gum arabic (see
   Glossary)
1 pinch saffron
2 tablespoons unsalted butter
1 teaspoon chives
Kosher salt to taste

**Garnish:**
½ ounce gold leaves
   (see Glossary)

**Preparation:** 5 minutes

**Cooking:** 10 minutes

Serves 4

**Method:**

For a luxurious and astonishing presentation, slice the tops from the eggshells, pour the eggs into a bowl, and set 4 eggshells in silver egg cups.

Combine egg, gum arabic, saffron, and chives in a bowl and whisk. In a nonstick pan, melt the butter over medium heat and pour in the egg mixture. Stirring constantly, softly scramble the eggs. Cook for 3 to 5 minutes, making sure the egg mixture doesn't stick to the bottom of the pan. When the eggs become creamy, season with salt.

Using a spoon, fill each of the eggshells, sprinkle with cumin, and top with gold leaves. Serve at once.

# Salads

# Red and Yellow Beet Salad with Goat Milk Feta, Sheep Milk Feta, White Balsamic Glaze, and Vanilla Bean Oil

This salad is simple, yet complex in flavors. The sweetness of roasted beets and the saltiness of both fetas balance well with the white balsamic glaze and the unique flavor of vanilla bean oil.

1 cup white balsamic vinegar

1 tablespoon organic honey

2 organic red beets

2 organic yellow beets

1 tablespoon kosher salt

2 tablespoons olive oil

4 ounces goat milk feta, cubed

4 ounces sheep milk feta, cubed

2 tablespoons vanilla bean oil (see Basics)

**Garnish:**

Microgreens

**Preparation:** 15 minutes

**Cooking:** 45 minutes to 1 hour

Serves: 4

**Method:**

In a small copper pot, bring vinegar and honey to a boil. Reduce by half. Remove from heat and cool at room temperature.

Wash red and yellow beets carefully without puncturing the skin. Season each beet with kosher salt and ½ tablespoon of olive oil. Wrap in foil and roast in a 375°F oven until tender, about 45 minutes to 1 hour. To check if beets are ready, insert a small knife in the center; if they are done, the knife will slide in easily.

Unwrap the beets and let them cool. Peel the skins and slice each beet into ½-inch rounds. Arrange both red and yellow beets on a serving dish. Place 1 ounce of both fetas between the red and the golden beets, drizzle each stack with ½ teaspoon of balsamic glaze and ½ tablespoon of vanilla bean oil. Garnish with microgreens.

# Cucumber Salad with Rose Water Vinaigrette and Fresh Mint

The use of fragrant rose water in the vinaigrette takes this simple cucumber salad to a new gastronomic level.

4 European cucumbers

2 tablespoons white balsamic
   vinegar

2 tablespoons rose water

2 teaspoons granulated sugar

6 tablespoons extra-virgin
   olive oil

1 tablespoon flat-leaf parsley,
   chopped

Kosher salt to taste

Freshly ground black pepper
   to taste

2 shallots, julienned

**Garnish:**

1 sprig fresh mint

**Preparation:** 20 minutes

Serves 6

**Method:**

Peel cucumbers, remove the seeds, and cut cucumbers into medium-size chunks. Set aside.

In a medium bowl, whisk together vinegar, rose water, and sugar. Slowly add olive oil until fully incorporated. Add parsley and season with salt and pepper.

To serve, mix the chopped cucumber and julienned shallots in a bowl. Toss with the rose water vinaigrette. Chill for 1 hour before serving, garnish with fresh mint.

# Zahlouk (Cooked Eggplant Salad)

Zahlouk is a traditional Moroccan salad, North Africa's version of ratatouille. This recipe was inspired by childhood memories of my mom's and grandma's versions.

2 eggplants, peeled and cubed
2 tablespoons olive oil
1 small yellow onion, diced
3 garlic cloves, minced
3 ripe tomatoes, peeled and
  coarsely chopped
½ tablespoon ground cumin
1 teaspoon paprika
2 tablespoons chopped fresh
  cilantro
Kosher salt to taste
Freshly ground black pepper
  to taste
Juice of ½ lemon

**Garnish:**
4 flat breads (see page 70)
1 cup cured black olives

**Preparation:** 15 minutes

**Cooking:** 35 minutes

Serves 4

**Method:**

Place eggplant cubes in a steamer and steam for 8 to 10 minutes or until soft. Transfer the eggplant to a cutting board and mash with a wooden spoon.

In a medium skillet, heat olive oil over medium heat, add onion and minced garlic, and cook for 5 minutes. Add tomatoes, eggplant, cumin, and paprika and cook over low heat for 20 to 25 minutes, or until all the liquid evaporates.

Add chopped cilantro, salt, and pepper, and stir in the lemon juice. Serve at room temperature or chilled, with flat bread and cured black olives on the side.

**Note:** The eggplant can be baked, steamed, or fried.

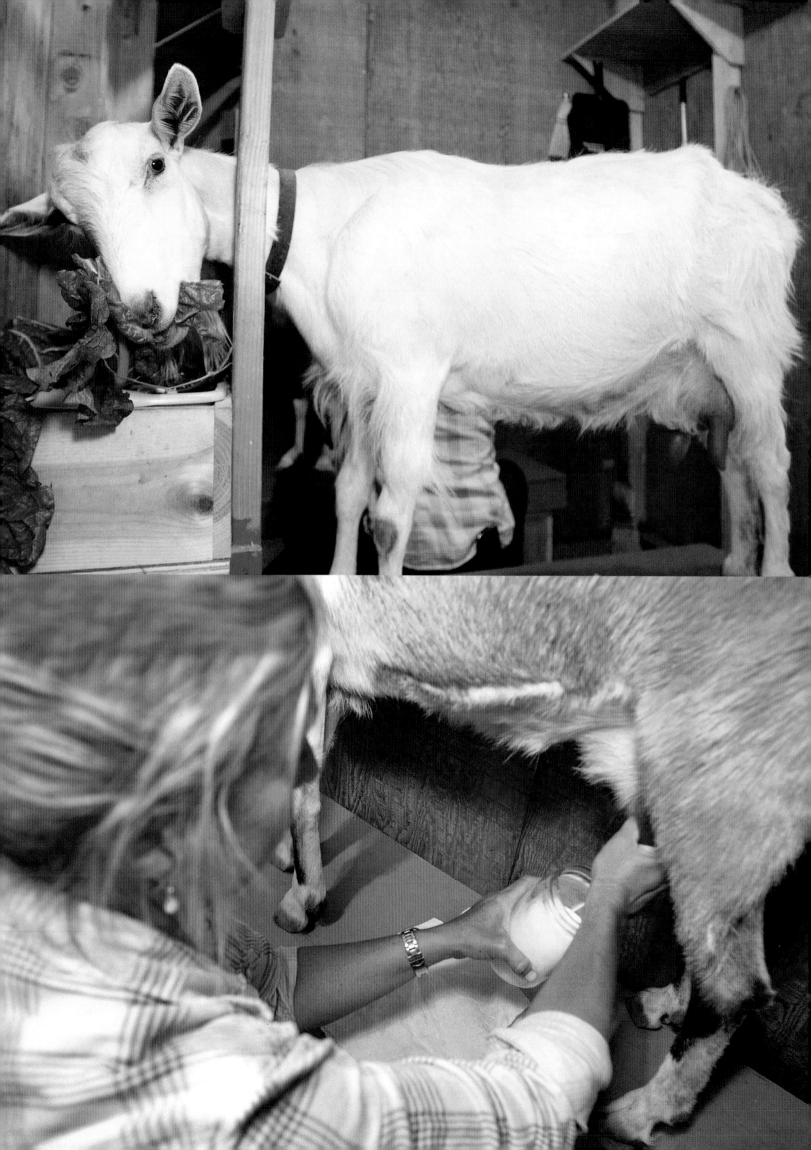

# Seafood, Fresh Seaweed, and Lollo Rosso Salad

This decadent millionaire salad is the perfect starter for a special meal. The rich sea urchin and sweet fresh scallops are offset by the saltiness of salmon roe and the fresh ocean taste of mackerel. The preserved lemon adds a unique balance to the dish.

2 fresh mackerel, skinned and deboned
4 diver scallops
4 ounces lollo rosso lettuce
2 ounces fresh seaweed
2 tablespoons extra-virgin olive oil
2 tablespoons lemon juice
4 tablespoons green olives, pitted and sliced
4 cherry tomatoes (red and yellow, cut in half)
Sea salt
Freshly gound black pepper
4 ounces fresh sea urchin
4 radishes, julienned

**Garnish:**
2 tablespoons salmon roe
2 ounces radish sprouts
¼ preserved lemon (rind only), julienned

**Preparation:** 20 minutes

Serves 4

**Method:**

Cut each mackerel into 6 pieces, set aside. Slice each diver scallop into 3 thin slices. Rinse the lettuce and seaweed well and drain.

In a medium bowl, gently toss the lettuce, sliced scallops, and seaweed with olive oil and lemon juice. Add olives and tomatoes. Season with sea salt and pepper.

Arrange lettuce, seaweed, and 3 slices of scallops in the center of each plate. Spoon olives and tomatoes on top. Lay 3 dollops of fresh sea urchin and 3 pieces of fresh mackerel around each plate. Arrange radishes in between pieces of seafood.

Garnish the salad with salmon roe, radish sprouts, and preserved lemon.

# Organic Mixed Greens, Granny Smith Apples, and Toasted Walnuts with Quince Vinaigrette

A simple salad with wonderful ingredients. Argan oil adds
a subtle nutty flavor to the quince vinaigrette.

8 ounces organic mixed greens

2 Granny Smith apples

1 cup walnut halves

**Quince Vinaigrette:**

2 tablespoons organic quince
  jam

2 tablespoons sherry vinegar

6 tablespoons olive oil

1 teaspoon argan oil
  (see Glossary)

Kosher salt to taste

Freshly ground black pepper

**Garnish:**

½ cup shaved pecorino Romano

**Preparation:** 25 minutes

Serves 4

**Method:**

Wash greens with cold water, place in a salad spinner, and spin. Pat dry with paper towel. Peel, core, and julienne the apples.

In a medium bowl, whisk together the quince jam and sherry vinegar. Slowly add olive oil and argan oil until fully incorporated. Season with salt and pepper. In the meantime, toast the walnuts for 5 minutes at 350°F.

In a salad bowl, combine the greens, apples, and toasted walnuts. Toss gently with 2 tablespoons of quince vinaigrette, or to taste. Garnish with shaved pecorino Romano. Serve extra vinaigrette on the side, if desired.

**Note:** If argan oil is not available, substitute French walnut oil.

# Chopped Salad with Orange Blossom Vinaigrette

Adding the fragrance of orange blossom to the vinaigrette takes this salad to a new level of sophistication.

2 fennel bulbs, julienned

1 tablespoon lemon juice

2 yellow beets

2 red beets

2 European cucumbers, peeled, seeded, and julienned

8 ounces baby heirloom tomatoes, halved

6 radishes, quartered

4 shallots, peeled and julienned

**Orange blossom vinaigrette:**

2 tablespoons sherry vinegar

1 tablepoon white balsamic vinegar

1 tablespoon orange blossom water

½ teaspoon granulated sugar

4 tablespoons grapeseed oil

4 tablespoons extra-virgin olive oil

Kosher salt to taste

Freshly ground black pepper to taste

1 tablespoon flat-leaf parsley, chopped

1 tablespoon orange zest

**Preparation:** 45 minutes to 1 hour

Serves 4

**Method:**

Place fennel in a small bowl with cold water and 1 tablespoon of lemon juice. Wash the yellow and red beets carefully without puncturing the skin. Wrap the beets individually in foil and roast in a 375°F oven until tender, about 45 minutes to 1 hour. Peel the beets, julienne, and set aside to cool. Prepare and cut cucumbers, tomatoes, radishes, and shallots.

To make the vinaigrette, in a medium bowl, whisk together the sherry vinegar, white balsamic vinegar, orange blossom water, and sugar. Slowly add the grapeseed oil and olive oil until fully incorporated. Season with salt and pepper. Just before serving, mix in chopped parsley and orange zest.

To serve, divide the vegetables among four plates. Drizzle with vinaigrette and serve at once.

# Baby Heirloom Tomatoes with Sherry Vinaigrette, Radish Sprouts, and Shaved Manchego Cheese

A baby heirloom tomato salad makes a wonderful first course. In this version, the sweet tomatoes are well balanced by a tangy sherry vinaigrette and mild manchego cheese.

8 ounces baby heirloom
   tomatoes
2 shallots, julienned
Pinch of sea salt
2 ounces radish sprouts
1 cup shaved manchego cheese

**Sherry vinaigrette:**

1 tablespoon sherry vinegar
1 teapsoon white balsamic
   vinegar
1 teaspoon grapeseed oil
3 tablespoons extra-virgin
   olive oil
Kosher salt to taste
Freshly ground black pepper
   to taste
1 teaspoon flat-leaf parsley,
   chopped
1 tablespoon cilantro, chopped

**Preparation:** 15 minutes

Serves 4

**Method:**

Wash the baby heirloom tomatoes and cut them in half. Place the tomatoes and julienned shallots in a bowl; season with sea salt.

In a medium bowl, whisk together sherry vinegar and white balsamic vinegar. Slowly add the grapeseed oil and olive oil until fully incorporated. Season with salt and pepper. Add the chopped herbs and mix well to combine.

Gently toss the heirloom tomatoes and shallots with the vinaigrette. Transfer to a plate, top with radish sprouts, and garnish with shaved manchego cheese. Serve at once.

# Baby Romaine Lettuce, Rosemary-Marinated Goat Cheese, and Tomato Jam with Cured Black Olive Vinaigrette

Baby romaine is complemented by the sharp flavor of cured black olive vinaigrette, while the tomato jam acts as the perfect match to the delicate, rosemary-marinated goat cheese.

1 goat cheese log, cut in 6 slices

2 garlic cloves, halved

2 sprigs fresh rosemary

2 cups extra-virgin olive oil, divided

6 heads baby romaine (red or green)

6 tablespoons tomato jam (see Basics)

1 French baguette, sliced and toasted

**Black olive vinaigrette:**

½ cup cured black olives, pitted

1 shallot, diced

1 teaspoon Dijon mustard

2 tablespoons balsamic vinegar

6 tablespoons olive oil

1 tablespoon flat-leaf parsley, chopped

Freshly ground black pepper to taste

**Preparation:** 25 minutes

Serves 6

**Method:**

To marinate the goat cheese log, place the goat cheese slices in a bowl. Add the garlic, rosemary, and 1 cup of olive oil. Cover and marinate in the refrigerator for at least 24 hours.

To make the vinaigrette, combine the olives, shallots, mustard, and vinegar in a blender; puree well. Slowly add 1 cup of olive oil while the blender is still running to make an emulsion. Add the parsley and season with pepper.

Wash the baby romaine, drain, and pat dry with a paper towel.

To serve, arrange 1 baby romaine lettuce head on each plate. Drizzle with 1 teaspoon of vinaigrette. Place 1 tablespoon of tomato jam on the same plate and top with 1 slice of marinated goat cheese. Serve with toasted baguette slices on the side.

# Octopus and Arugula with Garlic Chips

Octopus salad with a lemon vinaigrette is accompanied by crispy garlic chips.

2 pounds octopus

Kosher salt to taste

2 tablespoons sherry vinegar

Juice of 2 lemons

2 tablespoons red wine vinegar

2 garlic cloves, minced

1 cup + 1 tablespoon
   extra-virgin olive oil

Freshly ground black pepper
   to taste

½ bunch flat-leaf parsley, finely
   chopped

8 ounces arugula

2 shallots, julienned

**Garnish:**

4 garlic cloves, thinly shaved
   (fried)

**Preparation:** 15 minutes

**Cooking:** For octopus, 45 minutes to 1 hour

Serves 8

**Method:**

Clean the octopus by removing the eyes, beak, and ink sac (or ask your fishmonger to clean it). Wash very well under running cold water, making sure all the sand is removed from the suckers. Bring a large pot full of water to a boil. Add salt, sherry vinegar, and octopus and cook for about 45 minutes to an hour. (It is very important to cook the octopus until tender. To test for tenderness, use kitchen shears to cut off a piece from the thick part of the tentacle and taste it.) Remove the octopus from the boiling water, or leave it to cool in the water to ensure that the octopus will be very tender. Rub the octopus lightly with a clean towel to remove any loose skin. Using a sharp knife, cut the octopus into ¼-inch slices. Chill for 2 hours.

In a medium bowl, whisk together the lemon juice, red wine vinegar, and garlic, then whisk in 1 cup of olive oil. Season with salt and pepper and add parsley. Reserve 2 tablespoons of vinaigrette and set aside.

Gently toss the chilled cooked octopus in the remaining vinaigrette, then refrigerate for 30 minutes to allow the flavors to settle. In a small sauté pan, heat 1 tablespoon of olive oil and fry the thinly shaved garlic into chips.

Mix the arugula and julienned shallots with the reserved 2 tablespoons of vinaigrette. Arrange the octopus and arugula on plates, sprinkle with garlic chips, and serve at once.

# Orange and Fennel Salad with Orange Blossom–Citrus Vinaigrette

This is a refreshing salad that has a combination of unique elements:
the licorice taste of fennel, the sweetness of navel oranges, and the astonishing
aroma provided by orange blossom water in the citrus vinaigrette.

2 navel oranges

2 large fennel bulbs

1 tablespoon lemon juice

2 shallots, julienned

**Orange blossom citrus vinaigrette:**

1 whole grapefruit

1 whole orange

1 whole lemon

1 teaspoon orange blossom water

1 tablespoon white balsamic vinegar

1 tablespoon granulated sugar

3 tablespoons extra-virgin olive oil

Kosher salt to taste

Freshly ground black pepper to taste

**Garnish:**

½ cup cured black olives

Flat-leaf parsley sprigs

**Preparation:** 30 minutes

Serves 4

**Method:**

Make the vinaigrette. Wash grapefruit, orange, and lemon well in cold water, cut in quarters, and remove the seeds. Place the citrus quarters in a blender and puree until smooth. Strain through a fine sieve, reserve the citrus liquid, and set aside. In a blender, combine the citrus liquid, orange blossom water, white balsamic vinegar, and sugar and blend. While the blender is still running, slowly add the olive oil to make an emulsion. Season with salt and pepper.

Peel 2 navel oranges, remove all the white pith, and cut into thin slices. Discard any seeds. Wash the fennel bulbs, remove any brown outer leaves, and cut the fennel into thin slices. Place in a bowl of cold water with the lemon juice.

To serve, place the sliced fennel and julienned shallots in a serving dish, top with orange slices, and drizzle with orange blossom–citrus vinaigrette. Chill for 30 minutes. Garnish with cured black olives and parsley. Serve at once.

# Green and White Asparagus Salad with Lavender Vinaigrette, Parmesan Crisp, and Poached Duck Egg

Contrasting green and white asparagus are paired with a lavender vinaigrette, topped off with the richness of poached duck egg.

12 white asparagus spears

12 green asparagus spears

2 cups Parmesan cheese, shredded

4 duck eggs

1 tablespoon white balsamic vinegar (see Glossary)

4 tablespoons lavender vinaigrette (see Basics)

Freshly ground black pepper to taste

**Garnish:**

Fresh lavender flowers

**Preparation:** 30 minutes

**Cooking:** 20 minutes

Serves 4

**Method:**

Cut the tough ends from the asparagus spears. Using a vegetable peeler, peel each asparagus from below the tip to the end. Wash the asparagus in cold water. Bring a medium pot full of water to a boil, add the asparagus, and blanch for 2 to 3 minutes. Remove from the water with a slotted spoon, then refrigerate.

Make the Parmesan crisp. On a nonstick baking sheet, spread 2 cups of grated Parmesan cheese into 4 rounds, ½ cup each. Bake at 375°F for 10 to 15 minutes, until the rounds are melted and slightly brown. The cheese will crisp up as it cools.

Poach the duck eggs. Bring a medium pot of water to a boil and add the vinegar. Break an egg into the water, then simmer for a few minutes until the egg white is set and the yolk is still soft. Repeat the process until all the eggs are poached. Remove with a slotted spoon and drain on a paper towel.

To assemble, arrange 3 white and 3 green asparagus spears in 2 layers on each plate. Place a Parmesan crisp in between the green and white asparagus. Top each plate with a poached duck egg and drizzle with 1 tablespoon of lavender vinaigrette. Sprinkle with pepper and garnish with fresh lavender flowers.

# Poultry and Game

# Chicken Bastilla (Sweet and Savory Pie)

This classic dish is a part of Moroccan culinary history. Traditionally it is served as a first course during feasts and weddings. Although time consuming and expensive, it is worth every penny. I often make this luxurious dish on special occasions for my family members and guests. Their first expression, once they taste it, is "heaven on earth."

**Fillings:**

1 whole chicken (3 pounds)
4 garlic cloves, minced
1 yellow onion, grated
1 teaspoon ground ginger
½ teaspoon ground turmeric
Pinch of saffron
2 cinnamon sticks
½ cup flat-leaf parsley, chopped
2 tablespoons cilantro, chopped
1 tablespoon kosher salt
½ cup unsalted butter

Juice of 1 lemon
10 eggs, beaten
Freshly ground black pepper
  to taste

**Almond mixture:**

1 tablespoon vegetable oil
3 cups blanched almonds
1 cup powdered sugar
2 teaspoons ground cinnamon

1 cup unsalted butter, melted
8 sheets phyllo dough

**Garnish:**

2 tablespoons powdered sugar
1 teaspoon ground cinnamon

**Preparation:** 1 hour
**Cooking:** 1 hour, 30 minutes
Serves 12 to 15

**Method:** Wash the chicken well with cold water. Pat dry and cut into quarters. Place the chicken quarters in a large pot with the garlic, onion, ginger, turmeric, saffron, cinnamon sticks, parsley, cilantro, and salt. Add ½ cup of butter, then cover with water. Bring to a boil, cover, and simmer for 1 hour and 30 minutes.

Make the almond mixture. In a medium skillet, heat oil and brown the almonds lightly. Drain on a paper towel. Once they are cool, coarsely grind the almonds. Place in a medium bowl and combine with sugar and cinnamon. Set aside.

Remove the cooked chicken quarters with a slotted spoon; set them aside to cool. Discard the cinnamon sticks. Over high heat, bring the cooking liquid to a boil, uncovered. Reduce the sauce until all the liquid evaporates. Meantime, remove all the bones and skin from the chicken quarters, shred the meat, and set aside.

Degrease the sauce with a ladle. Once all the liquid evaporates, add the lemon juice and beaten eggs. Stir constantly until the eggs are cooked; season with salt and pepper and set aside.

Heat 1 cup of unsalted butter, then discard the milky solids. Set 8 stacked phyllo sheets on a cutting board, placing a damp paper towel on top to prevent them from drying out. Brush the bottom of an 11-inch cast-iron skillet with melted butter. Layer 4 phyllo sheets on the bottom of the skillet, leaving a 1½-inch border of phyllo dough extending up the sides of the pan. Brush each sheet lightly with butter. Build the bastilla in 3 layers: first place the shredded chicken on the bottom, layer it with the cooked egg, and top it with the almond mixture. Fold over the edges to partially cover the filling. Place 2 sheets of phyllo dough on top of the filling and tuck them under the bastilla to stay firm. Brush with melted butter. To make a 5-inch pie, use the same process with a 5-inch cast-iron skillet. Preheat the oven to 400°F. Bake the bastilla until golden brown, 20 to 25 minutes. Place the bastilla on a large serving platter, dust the top with powdered sugar, and run crisscross lines of ground cinnamon over the top. Serve hot.

# Argan Oil

Organic, First Cold Press
Extra Virgin

ARGANUSA

Net Wt. 150 ml (5.1 oz)

# Roasted Organic Chicken with Aged Butter and Saffron

Poultry is an essential meat in Moroccan cuisine. The use of smen (aged butter) adds a unique flavor and aroma to the dish. It takes you back centuries to the countryside of Berber tribes, where smen originated.

---

1 organic whole chicken
  (3 pounds)
Kosher salt
3 garlic cloves
2 pinches saffron (pulverized)
1 teaspoon ground turmeric
Freshly ground black pepper
  to taste
1 yellow onion, chopped
2 bay leaves
2 teaspoons smen (aged
  butter) (see Glossary)

**Preparation:** 15 minutes
**Cooking:** 1 hour

Serves: 6

**Method:**

Wash the chicken with cold water mixed with 1 tablespoon of kosher salt; pat dry. Pound 3 garlic cloves into a paste, then rub it into the flesh and cavity of the chicken. Let the chicken stand for 1 hour, then wash it well with cold water.

Soak 2 pinches of pulverized saffron threads in 1 cup of hot water and mix in the turmeric; set aside to cool. Place the chicken in a roasting pan, season with salt and pepper. Stuff the chicken cavity with chopped onion mixed with bay leaves. Pour the saffron water over the chicken to coat evenly. Melt 2 smen and brush it all over the chicken. Preheat the oven to 375°F. Roast the chicken for 1 hour, basting 3 to 5 times with juices in the roasting pan, until the chicken is tender.

Pour the juices from the cavity into the roasting pan, then place the roasted chicken on a platter and keep it warm. Over medium heat, bring the cooking juices plus 1 cup of water to a boil. Skim off the fat, reduce by half. Strain and serve on the side with the roasted chicken.

# Free-Range Chicken with Sweet Tomato Jam and Marcona Almonds

This is a unique preparation for chicken. It is accompanied by a delicious tomato jam that is enhanced by the combination of organic honey and orange blossom water.

4 Airline chicken breasts
  (see Glossary)
2 tablespoons olive oil
2 teaspoons ground cinnamon,
  divided
1 pinch saffron (pulverized)
¼ teaspoon ground ginger
1 teaspoon sea salt
½ teaspoon freshly ground
  black pepper
2 garlic cloves, minced
3 pounds ripe tomatoes
½ cup grated onion
1 tablespoon tomato paste
3 tablespoons organic honey
2 tablespoons orange blossom
  water

**Garnish:**
½ cup marcona almonds

**Preparation:** 15 minutes + 24 hours to marinate

**Cooking:** 1 hour, 15 minutes

Serves 4

**Method:**

In a medium bowl, coat chicken breasts with the olive oil. Mix 1 teaspoon of cinnamon, saffron, ginger, sea salt, pepper, and garlic. Rub mixture into the flesh of the chicken breasts, cover, and refrigerate overnight. Meanwhile, peel tomatoes, remove the seeds, dice, and set aside.

After 24 hours, place the marinated chicken breasts in a casserole dish, add 2 cups of water and the grated onion, bring to a boil, and simmer uncovered for 25 minutes. Add the tomato paste and diced tomatoes. Cook over medium heat, turning the chicken breasts 3 to 5 times in the sauce until they become tender. Remove the cooked chicken breasts, cover, and keep warm.

Add 1 teaspoon of cinnamon to the tomatoes, then cook down over high heat until all the liquid evaporates. The tomatoes will start to fry in the oils released from the cooking process. Add honey and orange blossom water to the tomato jam. Stirring often to avoid scorching, continue cooking for 5 to 10 minutes, then season with pepper. To serve, spoon 1 tablespoon of sweet tomato jam over each chicken breast. Garnish with marcona almonds.

# Moorish Chicken Kebobs with *Ras el Hanout*

*Ras el hanout*, which translates as "top of the shop," is a unique spice blend that dates back centuries. Most Moroccan households have their own recipes that are passed down from generation to generation. *Ras el hanout* flavors this delicious and easy preparation of chicken kebobs.

2 pounds boneless chicken
  thighs
4 tablespoons olive oil,
  divided
3 garlic cloves, minced

**Ras el hanout:**
1 tablespoon ground cumin
2 tablespoons paprika
1 teaspoon ground cinnamon
½ teaspoon freshly ground
  black pepper
1 tablespoon kosher salt
1 tablespoon brown sugar
½ teaspoon nutmeg
1 tablespoon fennel seeds,
  lightly toasted

**Garnish:**
1 bunch flat-leaf parsley
6 flat breads (see page 70)
1 lemon (cut into wedges)
2 tablespoons harissa
  (see Basics)

**Preparation:** 30 minutes + 12 hours to marinate

**Cooking:** 10 to 15 minutes

Serves 6 to 8

**Method:**

In a small bowl, combine all the spices to create *ras el hanout*; set aside.

Trim any fat from the chicken thighs. Cut the meat into 1-inch cubes. Place the chicken pieces in a medium bowl. Toss with 2 tablespoons of olive oil, the garlic, and the spice mixture, making sure every piece is well coated. Cover and refrigerate for at least 12 hours.

Thread 6 to 7 cubes of chicken on large skewers. Grill the chicken kebobs over mesquite wood or charcoal for 8 to 10 minutes, turning the kebobs and basting with olive oil. Place the chicken kebobs on a platter, and garnish with fresh parsley. Serve with flat bread, lemon wedges, and harissa.

# Chicken Tagine with Preserved Lemon and Moroccan Green Olives

Tagine is one of the most popular recipes in the Moroccan culinary repertoire. Anyone who visits Morocco should taste this fragrant, exquisite dish.

4 chicken thighs

4 chicken legs

1 tablespoon kosher salt

2 tablespoons olive oil, divided

1 teaspoon ground ginger

½ teaspoon ground cumin

½ teaspoon ground cinnamon

Sea salt to taste

Freshly ground black pepper
  to taste

½ cup grated onion

3 garlic cloves, minced

1 pinch saffron

¼ preserved lemon (see Basics)

1 cup Moroccan green olives,
  pitted

1 tablespoon cilantro, chopped

1 tablespoon flat-leaf parsley,
  chopped

4 flat breads (see page 70)

**Preparation:** 15 minutes + 3 hours to marinate

**Cooking:** 1 hour

Serves 4

**Method:**

Wash the chicken pieces with cold water mixed with 1 tablespoon of kosher salt; pat dry. In a medium bowl, combine the chicken with 1 tablespoon of olive oil, ginger, cumin, and cinnamon; toss gently. Refrigerate for 2 to 3 hours.

In a medium casserole dish, heat 1 tablespoon of olive oil over medium heat and add the marinated chicken. Season with sea salt and pepper and cook for 3 to 5 minutes. Add the onion, garlic, saffron, and 2 cups of water. Bring to a boil, cover, and simmer for 45 minutes to 1 hour, turning the chicken pieces often in the sauce. Meanwhile, rinse the preserved lemon and julienne. Add green olives and the preserved lemon strips to the chicken. Continue cooking, uncovered, for 10 minutes. Taste, and add more salt if needed.

Transfer the cooked chicken pieces to a serving bowl and spoon the olives and lemon stips around them. Stir the cilantro and parsley into the sauce and pour over the chicken. Serve at once with flat bread on the side.

# Duck Two Ways: Almond-Crusted Duck Leg Confit with Organic Honey, and Rose-Marinated Duck Breast with Amlou

This is a delightful combination of textures and flavors. Argan oil, also known as "Moroccan liquid gold," gives the dish a unique nutty flavor.

**Duck leg confit:**

4 duck legs

4 tablespoons kosher salt

1 quart duck fat (found in specialty stores)

4 garlic cloves

2 bay leaves

1 sprig fresh thyme

1 cup Marcona almonds

**Rose-marinated duck breast:**

4 duck breasts

1 shallot, julienned

2 garlic cloves, chopped

1 teaspoon dried lavender

6 dried rosebuds

1 cinnamon stick

1 tablespoon olive oil

1 orange, quartered

Kosher salt to taste

Freshly ground black pepper to taste

**Garnish:**

2 tablespoons organic honey

4 tablespoons amlou (see Glossary)

2 teaspoons argan oil (see Glossary)

Rose petals

**Preparation:** 30 minutes + 24 hours to marinate

**Cooking:** 1 hour, 30 minutes

Serves 4

**Method:**

Place the duck legs on a cutting board. French each duck leg by removing the meat from the end of the leg, exposing the bone. Pack kosher salt underneath the meat. Transfer to a shallow pan, cover, and refrigerate overnight.

Make the marinade for the duck breast. In a medium bowl, combine the shallots, chopped garlic, lavender, rosebuds, cinnamon stick, olive oil, and orange wedges. Make 2 to 3 incisions to each duck breast using a sharp knife. Place the duck breasts in the rose marinade. Cover and refrigerate overnight.

Preheat oven to 280°F. Wash salt off the duck legs and pat dry with paper towels. Place the duck legs in a baking dish with the duck fat. Add the garlic, bay leaves, and fresh thyme. Cover and bake for 1 hour and 30 minutes, or until the duck legs are tender. Remove the cooked duck legs and set aside. Save the duck fat for future use.

Remove the duck breasts from the marinade. Season each duck breast with salt and pepper. Place duck breasts skin side down in a hot sauté pan. Sear over medium heat on each side for 3 to 5 minutes or until cooked medium rare. Let the meat rest for 3 minutes before slicing.

Coarsely grind the Marcona almonds. Coat each duck leg with almonds and broil for 3 to 5 minutes, until the almond crust is golden brown.

To assemble, place an almond-crusted duck leg confit on each plate and drizzle with ½ tablespoon of honey. Arrange slices of duck breast over 1 tablespoon of amlou, drizzle with argan oil, and garnish with rose petals. Serve hot.

# Meat

# Coriander and Rosemary–Scented Lamb Rack with Brown Lentil Salad

Lamb is frequently used in Moroccan cuisine and throughout the Mediterranean region. The combination of fresh rosemary and ground coriander elevates the flavor of the lamb chops, which are perfectly matched with a light lentil salad.

2 pieces rack of lamb (7 to 8 ribs each, Frenched)
5 garlic cloves, sliced
1 tablespoon ground cumin
3 tablespoons ground coriander
4 sprigs fresh rosemary
2 tablespoons olive oil
Kosher salt to taste
Freshly ground black pepper to taste

**Lentil salad:**
1 tablespoon olive oil
1 shallot, finely chopped
1 tomato, peeled, seeded, and finely chopped
2 cups cooked brown lentils
½ teaspoon ground cumin
½ teaspoon paprika
2 tablespoons flat-leaf parsley, chopped
Kosher salt to taste
Freshly ground black pepper to taste

**Garnish:**
Fresh rosemary sprigs

**Preparation:** 25 minutes + 2 hours to marinate

**Cooking:** 15 minutes

Serves 4 to 6

**Method:**

Trim any excess fat from the lamb racks and French cut down between the bones of each rack of lamb to create chops (about 4 double lamb chops from each rack). In a medium bowl, combine the lamb chops, garlic, 1 tablespoon of cumin, coriander, rosemary, and 2 tablespoons of olive oil, and toss gently. Cover and marinate for 2 to 3 hours.

For lentil salad, heat 1 tablespoon of olive oil in a medium pan, and sauté the shallot until translucent. Add tomato, cooked lentils, ½ teaspoon of cumin, and paprika, and cook for 5 to 10 minutes. Add parsley, season with salt and pepper, remove from heat, and set aside.

Preheat oven to 375°F. Remove the lamb chops from the marinade and season with salt and pepper. Place the lamb chops in a hot sauté pan and sear over medium-high heat for 3 to 5 minutes. Roast in the oven for 10 minutes or until cooked medium rare.

To serve, spoon a large amount of lentil salad on a plate. Place 2 double lamb chops on top and garnish with fresh rosemary. Serve hot.

# Braised Beef Short Ribs with Caramelized Pearl Onions and Moroccan Potato Salad

Caramelized onions complement braised meat that is cooked to perfection in this comfort dish. A light potato salad adds the final touch.

8 beef short ribs
Kosher salt
Freshly ground black pepper
1 cup flour
2 tablespoons grapeseed oil
1 onion, coarsely chopped
4 whole garlic cloves
1 tablespoon tomato paste
1 cup fresh grape juice
1 quart beef stock
2 cinnamon sticks
3 sprigs fresh thyme
2 bay leaves
24 pearl onions
2 tablespoons unsalted butter
1 tablespoon granulated sugar

**Potato salad:**

2 potatoes, boiled, peeled, and
   diced
2 tablespoons olive oil
½ teaspoon paprika
3 sprigs flat-leaf parsley,
   chopped
2 tablespoons fresh lemon juice
Kosher salt to taste
Freshly ground black pepper
   to taste

**Garnish:**
3 sprigs fresh thyme

**Preparation:** 30 minutes

**Cooking:** 2 to 3 hours

Serves 4

**Method:**

Preheat oven to 350°F. Season the beef short ribs with salt and pepper, dust in flour. Heat grapeseed oil over medium-high heat in a large roasting pan. Sear the short ribs for 3 minutes on each side or until golden brown. Remove the ribs and set aside. In the same roasting pan, sauté the chopped onion and garlic cloves until translucent. Add tomato paste and cook for 2 minutes. Add grape juice, beef stock, cinnamon sticks, thyme, and bay leaves. Return the short ribs to the roasting pan, cover, and braise in the oven for 2 to 3 hours or until meat is tender. Reserve the braising liquid, reduce, strain, and set aside.

In a small sauté pan, cook the pearl onions in unsalted butter over medium heat for 5 to 10 minutes. Add sugar and continue cooking until the onions are tender and golden brown. Season with salt and pepper. Set aside and keep warm.

In a small bowl, combine potatoes, olive oil, paprika, parsley, and lemon juice, tossing gently. Season with salt and pepper, cover, and chill.

To serve, arrange 6 caramelized pearl onions in the center of each plate. Place a couple of short ribs on top, spoon the potato salad on the side, and drizzle the plate with the reduced braising liquid. Garnish with fresh thyme, serve at once.

# Lamb Tagine with Apricots and Organic Honey

Moroccan cuisine is well known for its extensive repertoire of tagines. Among them are sweet tagines with fruits. In this recipe I pair the lamb with succulent apricots and organic honey.

2 pounds lamb shoulder
1 small onion, grated
1 teaspoon ground ginger
1 teaspoon ground cinnamon, divided
Pinch of Saffron (pulverized)
2 tablespoons olive oil, divided
Sea salt to taste
Freshly ground black pepper to taste
2 cups dry apricots
3 tablespoons organic honey

**Garnish:**
2 teaspoons toasted sesame seeds

**Preparation:** 30 minutes + 3 hours to marinate
**Cooking:** 2 hours

Serves 4

**Method:**

Trim any excess fat from the lamb shoulders, cut the meat into chunks, and place in a bowl with onion, ginger, ½ teaspoon of cinnamon, saffron, and olive oil. Season with salt and pepper. Toss gently, cover, and marinate for 2 to 3 hours.

Sauté the lamb chunks in a casserole dish with 1 tablespoon of olive oil over medium-high heat, to gently release the spices' aromas and lightly sear the meat. Add 2 cups of water, bring to a boil, cover, and reduce the heat and simmer for 1½ hours, turning the lamb chunks often.

Soak dried apricots in cold water for 10 to 15 minutes. Drain the apricots and add them to the lamb tagine. Stir in ½ teaspoon of cinnamon and the honey. Simmer uncovered for 10 to 15 minutes.

To serve, arrange the lamb in the center of each plate, pour the sauce over, and spoon the glazed apricots on top. Sprinkle with toasted sesame seeds.

# Maui Wildflower Honey

This raw, organic island honey is produced by the bees from a variety of floral sources depending on the time of year. To produce one pound of honey the bees may collectively fly 24,000 miles and visit from 3 to 9 million flowers. We take special care in bringing you this ambrosia from our home apiary.

## Aloha and Enjoy!

Mark Damon & Leah Wesson
150 Pulehu Nui Rd., Kula, Hi. 96790  808-280-6652
net wt. 48 oz. ( 3 pounds/1.36 kg. )
Do not feed honey to infants under one year of age

# Lamb Meatballs Tagine with Poached Organic Eggs

This dish, served in households throughout Morocco, is home cooking at its best. The combination of the spices and rosebuds with the lamb meatballs gives this simple dish its finest moment.

1 pound ground lamb
½ cup grated onion
3 garlic cloves, minced
1 teaspoon ground cumin
¼ teaspoon ground cinnamon
1 teaspoon paprika
½ teaspoon ground coriander
3 flat-leaf parsley sprigs, chopped
3 dried rosebuds (broken up)
Sea salt to taste
Freshly ground black pepper to taste
1 tablespoon olive oil
1 quart tomato sauce (see Basics)
5 organic eggs

**Garnish:**
5 cilantro sprigs, chopped
4 flat breads (see page 70)

**Preparation:** 15 minutes
**Cooking:** 35 minutes

Serves 4

**Method:**

In a medium bowl, combine the ground lamb with grated onion, garlic, cumin, cinnamon, paprika, ground coriander, parsley, and rosebuds. Season with salt and pepper. Knead until well mixed, cover, and let stand for 2 hours in the refrigerator.

Shape the ground lamb mixture into 1-inch meatballs.

Heat olive oil in a large nonstick frying pan over medium heat. Fry the meatballs until browned. Add the tomato sauce, bring to a boil, and cook for 5 minutes over medium heat. Lower heat and simmer for another 20 minutes.

Crack the eggs between the cooked meatballs, cover, and poach over low heat for 3 to 5 minutes or until the eggs are set. Garnish with chopped cilantro and serve hot with flat bread on the side.

# Braised Oxtail with Pomegranate Molasses, Golden Raisins, and Toasted Sesame Seeds

This flavorful braised oxtail with pomegranate pays tribute to the Moorish heritage.

1 tablespoon olive oil

3 to 4 pounds oxtail

1 onion, finely chopped

¼ teaspoon nutmeg

1 teaspoon paprika

Kosher salt to taste

Freshly ground black pepper
   to taste

1 (14-ounce) can diced
   tomatoes

1 quart chicken broth
   (see Basics)

3 tablespoons pomegranate
   molasses

4 tablespoons organic honey

1 cup golden raisins

**Spice sachet:**

2 bay leaves

2 cinnamon sticks

4 black peppercorns

3 fresh thyme sprigs

8 juniper berries

**Garnish:**

Golden raisins

2 tablespoons toasted sesame
   seeds

**Preparation:** 20 minutes

**Cooking:** 3 hours

Serves 6

**Method:**

Heat olive oil in a large pot over medium heat. Add the oxtail, onion, nutmeg, and paprika, and season with salt and pepper. Cook for 5 to 10 minutes until the oxtail is lightly browned.

While the oxtail cooks, make the spice sachet. Combine bay leaves, cinnamon sticks, peppercorns, thyme, and juniper berries in a piece of cheesecloth and tie with kitchen twine.

Add diced tomatoes, chicken broth, and the spice sachet to the oxtail. Cover and boil over high heat for about 1 hour. Reduce the heat to medium-low and add molasses and honey. Simmer uncovered for 2 hours or until the oxtail is very tender and all the liquid has evaporated.

Discard the spice sachet, add 1 cup of golden raisins, and cook for 5 more minutes.

To serve, transfer the braised oxtail to a large serving dish. Sprinkle with a few raisins and toasted sesame seeds. Serve hot.

# Lamb Kebobs with Mint-Tomato Relish

The Mediterranean region's kebobs are world renowned, and the recipes and meats used vary from country to country. Lamb kebobs are one of the most popular fast foods in Morocco. These are served with a mouthwatering mint-tomato relish that contrasts with the smoky flavor.

---

1 boneless leg of lamb
  (3 pounds)
3 tablespoons olive oil
1 yellow onion, grated
4 garlic cloves, minced
1 tablespoon ground cumin
2 teaspoons paprika
2 teaspoons ground coriander
3 fresh cilantro sprigs, chopped
3 flat-leaf parsley sprigs,
  chopped
4 tablespoons fresh lemon juice
Kosher salt to taste
Freshly ground black pepper
  to taste

**Mint-tomato relish:**
4 organic tomatoes, peeled,
  seeded, and chopped
3 green onions, roughly
  chopped
1 shallot, finely chopped
½ tablespoon granulated sugar
5 fresh mint leaves, sliced
Sea salt to taste
Freshly ground black pepper
  to taste

**Garnish:**
3 tablespoons ground cumin
5 flat bread pieces
  (see page 70)

**Preparation:** 45 minutes + 24 hours to marinate
**Cooking:** 10 minutes

Serves 8 to 10

**Method:**

Trim any excess fat from the leg of lamb and cut the meat into 1-inch cubes. In a large bowl, toss the lamb meat with olive oil, onion, garlic, cumin, paprika, coriander, cilantro, parsley, and lemon juice. Make sure every piece is well coated. Season with salt and pepper, cover, and refrigerate overnight.

In a small bowl, toss gently the tomatoes, green onions, shallot, sugar, and mint to make the relish. Season with sea salt and pepper. Refrigerate.

Thread 8 to 10 pieces of lamb on large metal skewers. Grill the lamb kebobs over mesquite or charcoal for 5 to 6 minutes on each side, or until cooked medium.

To serve, place the lamb kebobs on a large platter. Pass mint-tomato relish, ground cumin, and flat bread.

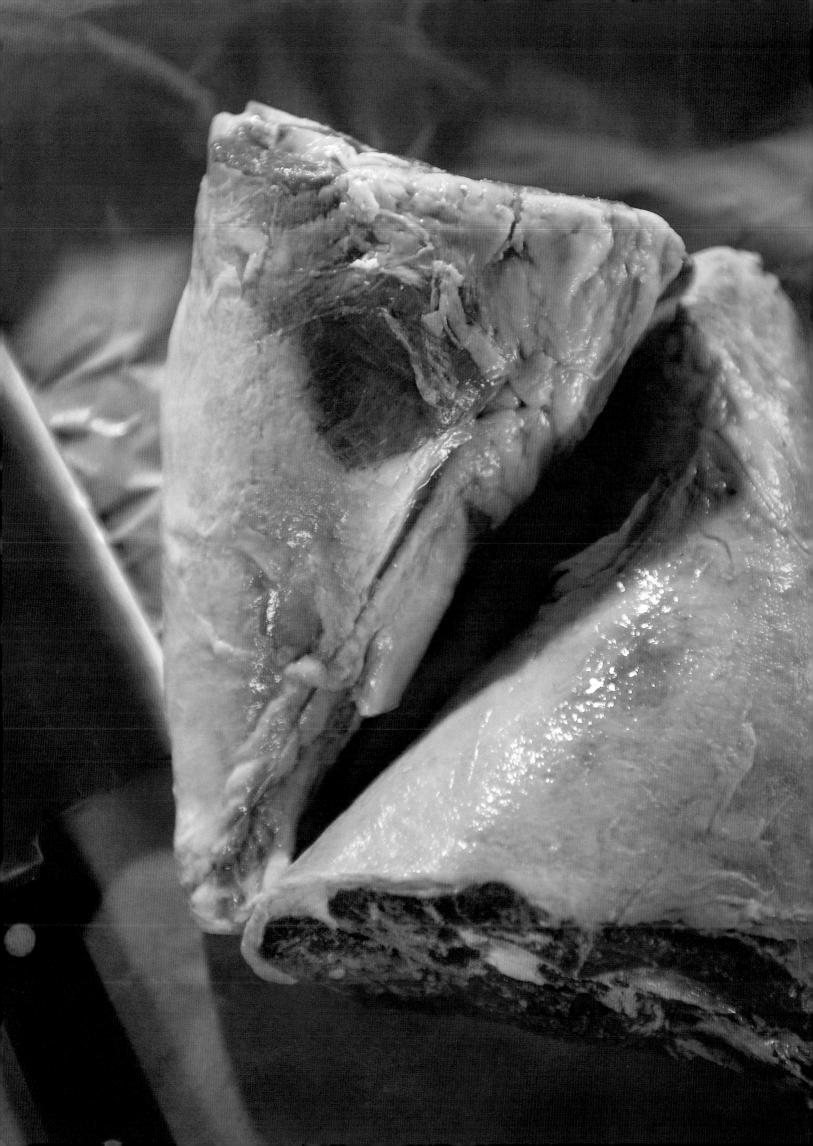

# Dry-Rub Beef Rib Eye with Porcini Mushrooms and Broccolini

This prime cut of beef is seasoned with an aromatic dry rub
and complemented with rich porcini mushrooms.

2 prime beef rib eye steaks
  (10 ounces each)
Kosher salt
Freshly ground black pepper
2 broccolini bunches
1 cup porcini mushrooms
2 tablespoons olive oil, divided

**Dry rub:**
3 tablespoons brown sugar
2 tablespoons paprika
1 tablespoon ground cumin
½ teaspoon ground cinnamon
¼ teaspoon allspice
1 teaspoon toasted fennel
  seeds
3 garlic cloves, minced

**Garnish:**
Pink peppercorns

**Preparation:** 45 minutes + 24 hours to marinate
**Cooking:** 10 minutes

Serves 2

**Method:**
Make the dry rub. In a small bowl, combine the brown sugar, paprika, cumin, cinnamon, allspice, fennel seeds, and garlic. Mix well and set aside.

Season the rib eye steak with salt and pepper. Work the spice rub into both sides of the meat, coating the rib eye completely. Cover and let stand for a minimum of 2 hours.

Bring a medium pot of water to a boil over high heat. Blanch the broccolini for a couple of minutes, remove from the water with a slotted spoon, and refrigerate.

Slice the mushrooms ¼-inch thick. Heat 1 tablespoon of olive oil in a small sauté pan over medium heat. Add the mushrooms and sauté for 3 to 5 minutes or until cooked. Season with salt and pepper; set aside and keep warm.

Grill the steaks for 5 to 7 minutes on each side or until cooked medium rare. Let the meat rest for 3 minutes. Meanwhile, heat 1 tablespoon of olive oil and sauté the broccolini for a couple of minutes until heated through; season with salt and pepper.

To serve, place the rib eye on a plate, top with porcini mushrooms, and spoon a couple of broccolini sprigs on the side. Garnish with pink peppercorns and serve hot.

# Couscous with Braised Lamb Shank and Seven Vegetables

Couscous is the national dish in Morocco. There are so many different ways of cooking couscous, depending on the region or tribe. According to tradition it must include at least seven vegetables. You can use lamb, beef, chicken, or fish.

1 pound lamb shoulder, trimmed and cut into small cubes

2 lamb shanks

Kosher salt to taste

Freshly ground black pepper to taste

4 tablespoons olive oil, divided

1 onion, diced

1 teaspoon ground ginger

1½ teaspoons ground turmeric

2 (10-ounce) cans diced tomatoes

½ bunch cilantro (tied with kitchen twine)

2 pinches saffron

1 (14-ounce) can chickpeas

1 green cabbage, quartered

2 carrots, peeled and cut into sticks

4 celery stalks, cut into sticks

4 turnips, peeled and cut in half

2 sweet potatoes, quartered

1 rounded tablespoon granulated sugar

4 zucchini, halved

1 pumpkin, quartered

4 cups couscous

4 cups water

1 tablespoon smen (aged butter) (see Glossary)

**Garnish:**

4 tablespoons harissa (see Basics)

**Preparation:** 45 minutes

**Cooking:** 2 hours and 45 minutes

Serves 6 to 8

**Method:**

Season the lamb shoulder and 2 lamb shanks with salt and pepper. Heat 2 tablespoons of olive oil in a large stockpot over medium heat. Add the onion and sauté until translucent. Add the seasoned lamb shoulder and lamb shanks and cook for 5 to 10 minutes, stirring often, until browned. Add the ginger, turmeric, tomatoes, cilantro, and 3 quarts of water. Bring to a boil and cook for 1 hour. Add the saffron, chickpeas, and cabbage, lower the heat to medium, cover, and cook for 45 minutes to 1 hour or until the lamb shoulder is tender. Transfer the lamb to an ovenproof dish, cover, and keep warm.

Add the carrots, celery sticks, and turnips to the soup broth, season with salt and pepper, and cook over medium-high heat for 15 minutes. Add the sweet potatoes and sugar and continue cooking for 10 minutes. Add the zucchini and pumpkin, cover, and cook for 15 to 20 minutes or until the pumpkin is done. Discard the cilantro and keep the soup broth and vegetables warm.

In a medium saucepan, bring 4 cups of water and 2 tablespoons of olive oil to a boil, and season with salt. Stir in the couscous, remove from heat, cover, and let stand for 5 minutes. Transfer the couscous to a medium bowl and fluff with 1 tablespoon of aged butter.

To serve, mound the couscous on a large serving platter, top with the lamb, and surround with the cooked vegetables. Serve with harissa and bowls of soup broth on the side.

# Lamb Tagine with Braised Artichoke Hearts, Green Olives, and Preserved Lemons

There are many variations of tagines. I choose to share one of my favorite dishes of all time, lamb tagine with artichoke hearts.

2 pounds lamb shoulder, cut into chunks

1 small onion, grated

3 garlic cloves, minced

1 teaspoon ground turmeric

1 teaspoon ground ginger

2 tablespoons olive oil, divided

Kosher salt to taste

Freshly ground black pepper to taste

Pinch of saffron (pulverized)

4 fresh artichokes

1 tablespoon fresh lemon juice

¼ preserved lemon, rinsed and cut into strips (see Basics)

½ cup Moroccan green olives, pitted

**Garnish:**

Chopped fresh parsley

**Preparation:** 30 minutes + 3 hours to marinate

**Cooking:** 2 hours

Serves 4 to 6

**Method:**

Trim any excess fat from the lamb shoulder. Place in a medium bowl with onion, garlic, turmeric, ginger, and 1 tablespoon of olive oil. Season with salt and pepper. Toss gently, cover, and marinate for 3 hours.

Heat 1 tablespooon of olive oil in a Dutch oven over medium heat. Sauté the marinated lamb chunks gently to release the spices' aromas, and lightly sear. Add the saffron, cover with 2 cups of water, and bring to a boil. Reduce the heat and simmer for 1 hour, turning the pieces of lamb often in the sauce. Add more water if needed.

Meanwhile, clean the artichokes by removing the leaves. Trim the base of each artichoke and remove the choke, leaving the stem on. Cut the artichoke in half and place in a bowl full of water with the lemon juice for 5 minutes.

Place the clean artichoke hearts over the cooked lamb in the Dutch oven. Add the preserved lemon strips. Cook for 30 to 45 minutes, or until the artichoke hearts are fully cooked. Add the olives to the lamb tagine and cook for 5 more minutes. Taste, and add more salt if needed.

To serve, place some lamb in the center of each plate, crisscross 2 half artichoke hearts beside it, spoon on olives, and drizzle the meat with the sauce. Garnish with fresh parsley and serve hot.

# Fish and Seafood

# Whole Sea Bream Tagine-Style with Yukon Potato, Poached Tomatoes, and Braised Celery

Morocco is renowned for its rich fishing grounds off the Mediterranean and Atlantic coasts. Roasted whole fish with vegetables is one of the most popular preparations throughout the country. Fish lovers will be delighted with this variation.

2 tablespoons cilantro, chopped

2 tablespoons parsley, chopped

1 bunch fennel tops, chopped

4 garlic cloves, minced

1 tablespoon paprika

1 teaspoon cumin

4 tablespoons lemon juice

3 tablespoons olive oil

Whole sea bream (3 to 5 pounds), cleaned and scaled

Sea salt to taste

Freshly ground black pepper to taste

1 pound celery sticks

1 onion, sliced

5 Yukon potatoes, sliced into 1-inch-thick rounds

4 tomatoes, skinned, seeded, and halved

3 bay leaves

**Garnish:**

Cured black olives

½ bunch flat-leaf parsley, chopped

Lemon slices

Flat bread (see page 70)

Harissa (see Basics)

**Preparation:** 45 minutes

**Cooking:** 30 minutes + 2 hours to marinate

Serves 6 to 8

**Method:**

Blend the cilantro, parsley, fennel tops, and garlic into a paste. Add paprika and cumin, stir in lemon juice and olive oil, mix well, and set aside.

Using a sharp knife, make 2 to 3 incisions to the sea bream. Season with salt and pepper. Rub the herb marinade into the cavity of the fish. Marinate for 2 hours in the refrigerator.

Peel the celery sticks. Arrange the celery sticks in one layer in a large roasting pan. Spread the sliced onion and potatoes over the celery in a single layer, then place the marinated sea bream on top. Arrange the tomato halves around the roasting pan and drizzle with the remaining herb marinade. Add the bay leaves. Cover with foil and bake in a 375°F oven for 35 to 45 minutes or until the fish is cooked through and the vegetables are done.

Garnish with olives, chopped parsley, and sliced lemon. Serve family-style with flat bread and harissa on the side.

# Lavender-Crusted Tuna with Saffron White Beans and Argan Oil

This recipe is inspired by the journey that brought me to this point in my life—the journey from Morocco to Maui. The meaty tuna is paired with saffron beans and topped with argan oil, also known as "Moroccan liquid gold."

5 flat-leaf parsley sprigs, chopped
1 ounce lavender
1 tuna loin (16 to 20 ounces)
Sea salt to taste
Freshly ground black pepper to taste
2 tablespoons grapeseed oil

**Saffron white beans:**
2 tablespoons olive oil
1 Maui onion, diced
3 garlic cloves, minced
2 pinches saffron (pulverized)
1 cup chicken broth (see Basics)
1 (16-ounce) can cannellini beans
Kosher salt to taste
Freshly ground black pepper to taste
2 tablespoons flat-leaf parsley, chopped
2 tablespoons cilantro, chopped

**Garnish:**
Rock salt
2 tablespoons argan oil (see Glossary)
Microgreens

**Preparation Time:** 20 minutes

**Cooking Time:** 2 minutes for the tuna

Serves 4

**Method:**

Make saffron white beans as follows. Heat olive oil in a large sauté pan over medium heat, add the onion and garlic, and cook for 5 minutes or until translucent. Add the saffron and chicken broth, bring to a boil, and cook for 5 more minutes. Lower the heat, stir in the beans, and simmer for 10 minutes, allowing the flavors to blend. Season with salt and pepper and remove from heat. Add parsley and cilantro to the saffron beans, mix well, and set aside at room temperature.

In a medium bowl, combine the 5 chopped parsley sprigs and lavender. Season the tuna loin with salt and pepper and roll in the lavender herb mix. Heat the grapeseed oil in a large skillet over high heat. Add the tuna loin and sear on all sides for 2 to 3 minutes or until cooked rare to medium rare. Let the tuna rest for 3 minutes.

To serve, cut the tuna loin into ¾-inch-thick slices. Spoon a good amount of saffron beans on each plate and top with 2 to 3 slices of rare tuna. Sprinkle the tuna slices with rock salt, drizzle with argan oil, and garnish with microgreens. Serve at once.

# Rosemary Skewer Prawns with Tropical Fruit Salsa and White Truffle Oil

Using rosemary sprigs as skewers adds a wonderful flavor to the prawns, which are accompanied by a refreshing tropical fruit salsa. This recipe is my version of fire and ice.

12 large shrimp, peeled and
　deveined
2 garlic cloves, minced
½ teaspoon ground cumin
½ teaspoon ground coriander
1 slice orange zest
2 tablespoons olive oil
Kosher salt to taste
Freshly ground black pepper
　to taste
4 large rosemary sprigs
　(for skewering)

**Tropical fruit salsa:**

1 mango, diced
2 kiwis, diced
½ pineapple, diced
1 strawberry papaya, diced
4 local strawberries, quartered
2 cane sugar cubes, crumbled
½ teaspoon white truffle oil

**Garnish:**

White truffle oil
Fresh mint sprigs

**Preparation:** 15 minutes + 1 hour to marinate

**Cooking:** 6 to 10 minutes

Serves 4

**Method:**

Place the shrimp in a medium bowl with the garlic, cumin, coriander, orange zest, and olive oil. Fold all the ingredients well, and season with salt and pepper. Cover and marinate for 1 hour in the refrigerator.

In a large bowl, combine the mango, kiwis, pineapple, papaya, strawberries, and sugar. Drizzle the white truffle oil on top and gently toss. Chill.

Preheat the grill. Thread 1 large shrimp onto each rosemary skewer. Grill over medium-high heat for 3 minutes on each side or until the shrimp are cooked through.

To serve, spoon a good amount of tropical fruit salsa on each plate. Place a rosemary skewer prawn on top. Drizzle with truffle oil, and garnish with fresh mint. Serve at once.

# Semolina-Crusted Hawaiian Red Snapper with Charmoula Sauce

Semolina flour gives the fish a fine crust. Charmoula sauce is commonly used in Moroccan fish dishes, as a sauce or as a marinade for a fish tagine.

4 red snapper fillets, 6 to 8
  ounces each (boneless)
Kosher salt to taste
Freshly ground black pepper
  to taste
2 cups semolina flour
4 tablespoons grapeseed oil

**Charmoula sauce:**

3 garlic cloves
½ cup flat-leaf parsley, chopped
½ cup cilantro, chopped
2 teaspoons paprika
1 teaspoon ground cumin
1 tablespoon sherry vinegar
4 tablespoons lemon juice
4 tablespoons olive oil

**Garnish:**

Lemon wedges
Fresh thyme

**Preparation:** 15 minutes

**Cooking:** 10 minutes

Serves 4

**Method:**

Make charmoula sauce. Using a mortar and pestle, crush the garlic, parsley, and cilantro into a paste. In a small bowl, combine the garlic and chopped-herb paste with paprika and cumin. Stir in the vinegar and lemon juice, then slowly stir in the olive oil. Season with salt and pepper and set aside.

Clean the snapper fillet and remove any fish bones with tweezers. Pat dry with a paper towel. Season the snapper fillets with salt and pepper and crust each one with semolina flour. Heat 2 tablespoons of grapeseed oil in a large sauté pan over medium-high heat. Place two snapper fillets skin side up and sear for 2 to 3 minutes on each side or until golden brown. Add 2 tablespoons of grapeseed oil for the second batch and repeat. Transfer the fish to a warm oven.

To serve, spoon a good amount of charmoula sauce on each plate. Place a snapper fillet on top, and garnish with lemon wedges and fresh thyme. Serve at once.

# Honey and Ginger–Coated Swordfish

The sweetness of honey and the sharp flavor of ground ginger
complement the meaty swordfish beautifully.

4 swordfish steaks (6 to 8
  ounces each)
Sea salt to taste
Freshly ground black pepper
  to taste
2 teaspoons ground ginger
1 teaspoon paprika
2 teaspoons olive oil
4 teaspoons organic honey
4 eggs, beaten
3 flat-leaf parsley sprigs,
  chopped
½ cup flour
2 tablespoons grapeseed oil

**Garnish:**
Organic honey
Pickled ginger
Apple cucumber slaw
  (see page 46)

**Preparation:** 2 hours to marinate

**Cooking:** 10 minutes

Serves 4

**Method:**

Season the swordfish steaks with salt and pepper. Sprinkle with
ginger and paprika, drizzle with olive oil, and spread 1 teaspoon
of honey on each swordfish steak. Cover and refrigerate for a
couple of hours.

In a medium bowl, combine the beaten eggs and the chopped
parsley. Dust each swordfish steak with flour, then coat on both
sides with the egg mixture. Heat grapeseed oil in a large sauté
pan over medium heat. Fry swordfish steaks for 3 to 5 minutes
on each side, depending on the thickness of the steaks, or until
the coating is golden brown and the steaks are cooked through.

Place a swordfish steak on each plate. Drizzle with honey,
garnish with pickled ginger, and serve with apple-cucumber
slaw on the side.

# Moorish Seafood Stew
# with Prawns and Diver Scallops

Saffron, cured black olives, and preserved lemon
give this seafood stew its Moorish personality.

---

2 tablespoons olive oil

1 Vidalia onion, diced

7 garlic cloves, minced
  (divided)

1 fennel bulb, julienned

Pinch of saffron

2 tomatoes, diced

2 cups tomato sauce
  (see Basics)

¼ cup cured black olives

¼ preserved lemon, sliced
  (see Basics)

6 large prawns, peeled and
  deveined

6 diver scallops

Kosher salt to taste

Freshly ground black pepper
  to taste

½ cup flour

2 tablespoons unsalted butter

**Garnish:**

½ bunch cilantro, chopped

**Preparation:** 15 minutes

**Cooking:** 30 to 35 minutes

Serves 4 to 6

**Method:**

Heat olive oil in a large sauté pan over medium heat, add the onion and half the amount of minced garlic, and cook until translucent. Add the fennel and continue cooking for 5 minutes. Add the saffron, tomatoes, and tomato sauce. Bring to a boil and cook for 10 more minutes. Lower the heat, add the black olives and preserved lemon, and simmer for 15 minutes. Season with salt and pepper and set aside.

Meanwhile, season the prawns and scallops with salt and pepper and dust lightly with flour. In a large skillet, melt the butter over medium heat, add the remaining garlic, prawns, and scallops, and cook for 3 to 5 minutes on each side or until the seafood is golden brown and firm to the touch.

To serve, spoon the sauce into a large serving platter. Place the scallops on top and arrange the prawns in between. Sprinkle with chopped cilantro and serve hot at once.

# Grilled Sardines with Anchovy Vinaigrette

Along the Mediterranean and the Atlantic coast cities in Morocco,
grilled fish is a favorite, especially sardines.

8 fresh sardines, cleaned and
   scaled
Sea salt to taste
2 tablespoons grapeseed oil

**Anchovy vinaigrette:**
½ shallot, minced
2 garlic cloves, minced
½ teaspoon ground cumin
½ teaspoon paprika
3 tablespoons sherry vinegar
8 tablespoons olive oil
4 anchovy fillets, chopped
5 flat-leaf parsley sprigs,
   chopped
Freshly ground black pepper

**Garnish:**
Fennel tops
Lemon wedges
1 cup caper berries
Fennel slaw (see page 82)

**Preparation:** 10 minutes

**Cooking:** 25 minutes

Serves 4

**Method:**

Make the anchovy vinaigrette. In a medium bowl, combine the shallot, garlic, cumin, paprika, and sherry vinegar, whisking constantly. Slowly add the olive oil until fully incorporated. Add the chopped anchovies and parsley. Season with pepper and chill.

Toss the sardines with a good amount of sea salt and chill for an hour. In the meantime, heat a barbecue grill. Brush the sardines with grapeseed oil and grill over medium-high heat for 2 to 3 minutes on each side, until the skin is charred and the fish is cooked through, turning the fish only once.

To serve, place the fennel tops on the bottom of a large platter, lay the grilled sardines on top, and garnish with lemon wedges and caper berries. Serve with anchovy vinaigrette and fennel slaw on the side.

# Basics

## CHICKEN BROTH

Yield: about 3 quarts

**Ingredients:**

2 pounds chicken bones and chicken wings

1 onion, chopped

2 carrots, chopped

2 celery stalks, chopped

1 leek, washed very well and chopped

2 bay leaves

5 whole white peppercorns

3 fresh thyme sprigs

3 flat-leaf parsley sprigs

3 garlic cloves

4 quarts cold water

**Method:**

Combine all ingredients with 4 quarts of water in a large stockpot. Bring to a boil, lower the heat, and simmer for 2 hours. Skim off the fat, strain, and reduce to about 3 quarts. Chicken broth can keep for up to
3 days.

## FENNEL BROTH

Yield: about 3 quarts

**Ingredients:**

2 fennel bulbs with tops, roughly chopped

1 tablespoon fennel seeds

2 bay leaves

4 parsley stems

4 quarts cold water

**Method:**

Combine all ingredients with 4 quarts of water in a large stockpot. Bring to a boil and simmer for 45 minutes. Strain and reduce to about 3 quarts. Chill and use according to recipe. The broth can keep for up to 5 days.

## HARISSA

Yield: about 1½ cups

**Ingredients:**

12 to 14 dried chilies

4 garlic cloves, minced

1 tablespoon ground cumin

1 cup extra-virgin olive oil

Kosher salt to taste

**Method:**

Split the dried chilies open and remove the seeds. Soak the chilies in warm water for 30 minutes.

Squeeze the water from the chilies. Place them in a blender with garlic, cumin, and olive oil. Puree until smooth and season with salt. Transfer the harissa into a mason jar and cover with a layer of olive oil. Harissa can keep for up to 6 months.

**Note:** Use kitchen gloves while handling chilies.

## LAVENDER VINAIGRETTE

Yield: about 1½ cups

**Ingredients:**

½ teaspoon culinary lavender

3 dry rosebuds

1 shallot, roughly chopped

3 tablespoons white balsamic vinegar

1 teaspoon organic honey

1 cup olive oil

Sea salt to taste

Freshly ground black pepper to taste

**Method:**

In a spice grinder, combine the culinary lavender and dried rosebuds and grind. Place the shallot and vinegar in a food processor and puree. While the food processor is still running, add the ground lavender and rosebud mixture. Add the honey and slowly pour in the olive oil. Season with sea salt and pepper and chill overnight. Shake well before using.

# Basics

## LEMON OLIVE OIL

Yield: 1 cup

**Ingredients:**

1 cup extra-virgin olive oil (first cold press)

½ cup lemon zest

**Method:**

Puree the olive oil and lemon zest together; refrigerate for 24 hours, then strain through a fine mesh.

## TOAST POINTS

Yield: 1 serving

**Ingredients:**

White bread

**Method:**

Take a slice of white bread, remove the crust, and slice on the diagonal to form four triangles. Place the triangles on a baking sheet and bake in a preheated 375°F oven for 4 minutes. Turn over and bake for another 2 minutes. Remove from the oven: the final products are toast points.

## LOBSTER BROTH

Yield: about 6 quarts

**Ingredients:**

5 pounds lobster shells (removed from bodies)

1 tablespoon olive oil

1 yellow onion, roughly chopped

5 celery stalks, roughly chopped

3 carrots, roughly chopped

1 leek, washed very well and roughly chopped

5 garlic cloves

2 (6-ounce) cans tomato paste

2 bay leaves

8 black peppercorns

5 flat-leaf parsley sprigs

¼ ounce fresh tarragon

5 fresh thyme sprigs

8 quarts cold water

**Method:**

Wash the lobster shells in cold water. Place in an ovenproof dish and roast at 375°F for 20 minutes. Meanwhile, in a large stockpot, heat olive oil over medium heat and caramelize the onion, celery, carrots, leek, and garlic together.

Add the tomato paste, bay leaves, peppercorns, parsley, tarragon, thyme, and the roasted lobster shells. Add the cold water, bring to a boil, and simmer over medium heat for 3 hours. Strain through a fine sieve and reduce to about 6 quarts. Store and use as directed in recipes. The broth can keep for 5 days in the refrigerator or up to 6 months in the freezer.

## VANILLA BEAN OIL

Yield: 1 cup

**Ingredients:**

1 (250-milliliter) bottle (about 1 cup) extra-virgin
   olive oil (first cold press)
2 vanilla bean pods

**Method:**

Split open the vanilla bean pods lengthwise. Using the tip of a paring knife, scrape the beans out of the pods.

Place both the vanilla beans and the pods into the olive oil bottle. Store in a dark, cool place. The vanilla bean oil will be ready after one week. Shake well before using.

## VEGETABLE BROTH

Yield: 3 quarts

**Ingredients:**

2 onions, chopped
4 celery stalks, chopped
2 carrots, chopped
1 leek, washed well and chopped
2 tomatoes, chopped
2 bay leaves
1 head of garlic
5 sprigs parsley
4 quarts cold water

**Method:**

Combine all ingredients with 4 quarts of water in a large stockpot. Bring to a boil and simmer for 1 hour. Strain and reduce to about 3 quarts.

# Basics

## PRESERVED LEMON

**Ingredients:**

8 Meyer lemons

1 cup rock salt, more if needed

16 black peppercorns

8 bay leaves

1 liter organic lemon juice

**Method:**

Wash the lemons well. Quarter the lemons from the top to almost ½ of the bottom of each lemon, making sure the quarters remain attached.

Stuff each lemon with rock salt and pack 2 lemons in each of 4 mason jars. Divide peppercorns and bay leaves among the jars. Top with lemon juice and seal the mason jars tight. Store in pantry for at least 6 weeks, shaking the jars each day to distribute the salt and lemon juice.

To use, rinse the lemons well under cold water. Preserved lemons will keep up to 1 year.

## TOMATO JAM

Yield: about 2 cups

**Ingredients:**

2 tablespoons olive oil

1 shallot, finely diced

4 garlic cloves, minced

5 pounds organic ripe tomatoes, peeled, seeded, and diced

2 pinches saffron

1 quart chicken broth (see page 184)

1 teaspoon pomegranate molasses

2 rounded tablespoons granulated sugar

Kosher salt to taste

Black pepper to taste

**Method:**

Heat olive oil in a medium sauté pan over medium heat. Add the shallot and garlic and cook for 5 minutes or until translucent. Add the tomatoes, saffron, and chicken broth. Cook over high heat. Halfway through the cooking process, add molasses and sugar. Continue cooking until all the liquid evaporates and the tomato jam is reduced by about half. Season with salt and pepper and chill before serving.

## MAUI ONION AND MEDJOOL DATE JAM

Yield: about 1½ cups

**Ingredient:**

½ cup orange juice

1 tablespoon orange blossom water

10 medjool dates, pitted and halved

1 tablespoon unsalted butter

2 Maui onions, finely diced

4 tablespoons grenadine

1 tablespoon lemon juice

1 tablespoon lemon zest

**Method:**

Combine the orange juice and orange blossom water in a medium bowl. Soak the dates in the liquid for about 20 minutes, then puree in the blender.

Meanwhile, heat butter in a medium sauté pan over medium heat. Add the onion and cook until translucent. Stir in the grenadine and continue cooking for 10 minutes. Add the dates and lemon juice and cook for 15 more minutes. Stir in the lemon zest. Cool the jam and store in a mason jar. The jam can keep for up to 2 weeks.

## MOORISH TOMATO SAUCE

Yield: about 2 quarts

**Ingredients:**

1 teaspoon olive oil

1 small Maui or Vidalia onion, chopped

4 garlic cloves

2 (14.5-ounce) cans organic diced tomatoes

½ teaspoon ground oregano

3 sprigs fresh thyme

2 quarts fennel broth

1 tablespoon granulated sugar

Sea salt to taste

Freshly ground black pepper to taste

**Method:**

Heat olive oil in a medium saucepan. Add the onion and garlic and cook for 10 minutes. Stir in tomatoes with their juice and cook for 20 minutes. Add oregano, thyme, and fennel broth and continue cooking for 45 minutes. Add sugar and puree. Season with salt and pepper, store, and use as directed in recipes. The sauce can keep for up to 7 days.

# Glossary

**Airline chicken:** A fancy cut of a chicken breast with the first wing segment "drumette" still attached.

**Amlou:** Amlou is a chunky paste, which some people compare to peanut butter. It is made with argan oil, almonds, and honey. It is popular among the Berbers and it orginated in Morocco, where argan oil is produced. Amlou can be difficult to obtain outside of Morocco, due to limited demand, and is best sought out in specialty stores.

**Argan oil:** This oil is produced from the kernels of the Argan tree, endemic to Morocco. It is valued for its nutritive, cosmetic, and numerous medicinal properties. The tree, a relict species from the Tertiary age, is extremely well adapted to drought and other environmentally difficult conditions of southwestern Morocco.

**Bastilla:** Bastilla, an elaborate meat pie, is traditionally made of squab (fledgling pigeons). Since squabs are often hard to get, shredded chicken is more often used today, though bastilla can also use fish as a filling. Highly regarded as a national dish of Morocco, this pie combines sweet and salty flavors: a combination of crisp layers of the crepe-like warka dough (a thinner cousin of phyllo); savory meat slow-cooked in broth and spices and shredded; and a crunchy layer of toasted and ground almonds, cinnamon, and sugar.

**Broccolini:** This green vegetable is similar to broccoli but with small florets and long, thin stalks. Broccolini's flavor is sweet, with notes of both broccoli and asparagus.

**Charmoula:** A marinade used in Moroccan cooking, charmoula is usually used to flavor fish or seafood, but it can be used on other meats or vegetables.

**Couscous:** A typical Berber food, couscous has become popular in many countries. Couscous granules are made by rolling and shaping moistened semolina wheat and then coating the grains with finely ground wheat flour. The finished granules are roughly spherical in shape and about one millimeter in diameter before cooking. Different cereals may be used regionally to produce the granules. Traditional couscous requires considerable preparation time and is usually steamed.

**Chickpeas:** Chickpeas (also known as garbanzo beans) have a delicious nutlike taste and buttery texture. They provide a good source of protein. They are available year-round, either dried or canned.

**Edible gold leaf:** Edible gold leaf has been used for decoration for centuries, most notably by the Italians and French. In Renaissance Italy, entire banquet dishes might be enveloped in gold. In 2009, the Japanese began decorating sweets with edible gold. Edible gold is appearing with greater frequency in fine dining, where restaurant chefs feel the need to present something unusual and evocative to their guests.

**Gum arabic:** Gum arabic, also known as gum acacia or meska, is a natural gum made of hardened sap taken from two species of the acacia tree. Gum arabic is a complex mixture of polysaccharides and glycoproteins, and is used primarily in the food industry as a stabilizer.

**Hamachi:** Also known as yellowtail, hamachi is a fish in the family Carangidae (a family that includes, pompanos, jack mackerels, and scads found in the Atlantic, Indian, and Pacific Oceans). It is greatly appreciated in Japan and often used in sushi.

**Harissa:** Harissa, originally from Tunisia, is a hot chili sauce commonly eaten in North Africa. Its main ingredients are piri piri chili peppers, serrano peppers, or other hot chilies and olive oil. Recipes for harissa vary according to the household and region. Variations can include the addition of cumin, red peppers, garlic, coriander, and lemon juice. In Sahara regions, harissa can have a smoky flavor. Prepared harissa is also sold in tubes, jars, and cans.

**Heirloom tomatoes:** Heirloom tomato (also called heritage tomato in the United Kingdom) is an open-pollinated (nonhybrid) heirloom cultivar of tomato. Heirloom tomatoes have become increasingly popular and more readily available in recent years.

**Lollo rosso:** This tender, mild variety of loose leaf lettuce has long leaves and ruffled edges that are green toward the interior of the head and red on the outer portion of the head.

**Manchego cheese:** Made in the La Mancha region of Spain from the milk of manchego sheep, this cheese is aged for between 60 days and 2 years. Manchego has a firm and compact consistency and a buttery texture, and often contains small, unevenly distributed air pockets.

**Marcona almonds:** Marcona almonds, the "queen of almonds," are imported from Spain. They are shorter, rounder, softer, and sweeter than the California variety.

**Maui onions:** Maui onions have long been considered among the best and most flavorful onions in the world. The Maui onion only grows in the deep red volcanic earth on the upper slopes of Haleakala, Maui's world-famous dormant volcano.

**Merguez:** (pronounced mer' gez, from the Berber *amergaz*, meaning sausage) A red, spicy sausage from North Africa, *merguez* is made with lamb, beef, or a mixture of both. It can be flavored with a wide range of spices, such as paprika, cayenne pepper, or harissa. It is stuffed into a lamb casing. It is traditionally made

fresh and eaten grilled. Sun-dried *merguez* is used to add flavor to tagines.

**Microgreens:** Microgreens are tender and tangy lettuce and mustard greens that are chopped off young, usually when they are only an inch or so high and barely a few weeks old.

**Moroccan green olives:** Moroccan picholine green olives are grown in the remote Atlas mountain range of Morocco, where the climate, rich soil, and ancient groves produce these savory olives. Today, the predominant variety of olive planted in Morocco is the picholine Marocaine, the cousin to the French picholine Languedoc. Given the milder and more consistent climate in Morocco, the picholine Marocaine grows into a superior table olive. The proof of this proposition is that France imports tons and tons of these olives to eat themselves and to export as a "product of France"—yes, most "French" picholines that are sold in the United States are in fact grown in Morocco.

**Moroccan cured black olives:** Ripe Moroccan picholine olives are the starting point for this traditional, centuries-old staple. Layers of olives are alternated with layers of salt, and the olives are left to cure for weeks. Wonderfully intense in aromatic flavor, they possess hints of black cherry and plum and have a slightly bitter finish. These wrinkled black olives remain meaty and full of deep, smoky qualities without being overly salty. Without a doubt, these are among the most flavorful ingredients in Moroccan cooking. Moroccan dry–cured olives are perfect for any use, from tabletop to cooking.

**Orange blossom water:** Orange blossom water is distilled water that contains the essential oils of the orange blossom. It is used in many lamb dishes and desserts, and is perfect for fruit. A little goes a long way, so add a few drops at a time to determine how

# Glossary

much you like. The blossoms of Seville oranges are believed to produce one of the finest orange blossom waters, since they have a strong, rich aroma.

**Pearl onions:** These mild-flavored red, white, or yellow skinned onions come in sizes of less than or a little more than 1 inch in diameter. Their flesh is white, and most often they are cooked to be served as a side dish or added whole to soups and stews.

**Phyllo dough:** Phyllo, paper-thin sheets of raw, unleavened flour dough, is used for making pastries in North African, Middle Eastern, Greek, and other regional cuisines.

**Pomegranate molasses:** Pomegranate molasses is a syrup-like reduction of pomegranate juice that has a unique, tart-sweet flavor and is a gorgeous, deep reddish purple color. It's as thick as maple syrup, with sweet and sour flavors that combine the best of balsamic vinegar with lush fruit. Great as an ingredient in an array of Middle Eastern dishes, it's the sort of addition to sauces and stews that adds enormous depth of flavor.

**Porcini mushrooms:** In the vast culinary world of edible mushrooms, only one can be called king. Italians affectionately call the porcini the ruling class of the delicious fungi. The meat-like texture of porcini, with its earthy, somewhat nutty flavor, is unequaled among mushrooms.

**Preserved lemons:** Preserved in a salt-lemon mixture (sometimes with spices such as bay leaf and black peppercorns) for about 30 days, these lemons have a silky texture and a distinctive flavor. They're an indispensable ingredient in Moroccan cooking and are used as a flavoring by many of today's leading chefs.

**Quince:** Quince has been around for centuries through-out Asia and the Mediterranean countries. This yellow-skinned fruit looks and tastes like a cross between an apple and a pear. Because of it high pectin content, it's particularly popular for use in jams and preserves.

**Ras el hanout:** Literally "Top of the shop," *ras el hanout* is a Moroccan spice blend that can contain more than 30 ingredients. For the Moroccan souks (spice merchants), it is a point of honor to have the most sought-after version of this blend. It is extremely versatile, adding an aromatic and enticing flavor to meats, fish, seafood, and vegetable tagines.

**Rose water:** Rose water was first produced by Muslim chemists in the medieval Islamic world through the distillation of roses, for drinking and perfumes. Rose water is the leftover liquid, or hydrosol, remaining when rose petals and water are distilled together for the purpose of making rose oil. Usage dates back to at least the early Romans, but production with steam distillation was probably first used by the Arabian doctor Avicenna in the 10th century.

**Saffron:** The Moors brought *az-safran* (the word means yellow) to Spain 1,000 years ago. Saffron appears in Moorish, Mediterranean, and Asian cuisines. Coming from the dried stigmas of the saffron crocus, it takes 75,000 blossoms or 225,000 hand-picked stigmas to make a single pound, which explains why it is the world's most expensive spice. Because of its expense, intense flavor, and strong dying properties, very little saffron is required for culinary purposes and the key is to distribute it evenly throughout the dish being prepared. It can be crushed to a fine powder with a mortar and pestle. It is easier, however, to steep the saffron in hot water—a pinch to a cup will create the desired flavor and color.

**Smen:** (also called sman) A traditional cooking oil commonly used in North African cuisines, smen is produced using the butter made from the milk of sheep or goat. The butter is boiled for about 15 minutes, then skimmed, strained into a ceramic jar called a *khabia*, and salted before it curdles. The resulting grease will then be aged, often in sealed containers buried in the ground. The older the smen, the stronger and more valued it becomes. Smen traditionally is used in the preparation of tagines. It holds great cultural significance, particularly as an indicator of familial wealth. As such, it will often be used as a token of honor for esteemed visitors to a household, akin to using the fine china or an especially prized wine in other cultures. Berber farmers in Morocco will sometimes bury a sealed vessel of smen on the day of a daughter's birth, aging it until it is unearthed and used to season the food served on that daughter's wedding day.

**Smoked salt:** Smoked salt lends a strong flavor and aroma to meats, vegetables, and seafood, and is suitable for vegetarians. Smoked salt differs from "smoke-flavored salt" in that the latter contains a smoke-flavored additive and is therefore not classified as a pure salt product. Smoked salt typically is made from evaporated sea salt, as opposed to mined salt.

**Sweet prawns:** This is a breed of sweet shrimp that is served in Japanese sushi. It usually comes accompanied with crunchy, deep-fried shrimp heads.

**Tagine:** This is a type of dish popular in North African cuisines, especially in Morocco. The traditional tagine pot is formed entirely of a heavy clay, which is sometimes painted or glazed. The pot consists of two parts: a base unit that is flat and circular with low sides, and a large cone or dome-shaped cover that rests inside the base during cooking. The cover is designed to promote the return of all condensation to the bottom.

With the cover removed, the base can be taken to the table for serving. Moroccan tagines are slow-cooked stews braised at low temperatures, resulting in tender meat with aromatic vegetables and sauce.

**Tedouira:** Harira is traditionally thickened with a type of sourdough starter called a *tedouira*. Water and flour are mixed together and sometimes left to ferment overnight. This mixture is then stirred into simmering soups and stews to give them a velvety consistency.

**Vidalia onion:** These onions were first grown near Vidalia, Georgia. The Vidalia is an unusually sweet variety of onion, due to the low amount of sulfur in the soil in which the onions are grown.

**White balsamic vinegar:** White balsamic vinegar blends white grape must with white wine vinegar and is cooked at a low temperature to avoid any darkening. Some manufacturers age the vinegar in oak barrels, while others use stainless steel.

**White truffle oil:** Truffle oil imparts the flavor and aroma of truffles to a dish. The white truffle comes from the Langhe area of the Piedmont region in northern Italy and, most famously, from the countryside around the city of Alba.

# Index

# Acknowledgments

It is a pleasure to express my appreciation to the people who supported me in any respect during the making and completion of *Moorish Fusion Cuisine*, first and foremost my father-in-law, Tadashi Kashiwabara, and my mother-in-law, Mieko Kashiwabara.

To my team, Alan De Herrera, Toni Gordillo, Adriana Hammond, and Tamara L. Kufman, my gratitude for their astounding professionalism.

**Alan De Herrera, food photographer,** is an accomplished travel and commercial photographer. Alan has spent his entire life chasing his dream of shooting the things he's most passionate about. He has always been fascinated with the technical and creative expertise required to shoot powerful images. His vast array of work over the years is impressive and his photos have been published in several newspapers and magazines.

In 2007, Alan started pursuing food photography and quickly fell in love with this new genre. "I was drawn to food photography in particular because of how challenging it is," says Alan. As with every great photograph, food portraits require excellent composition, amazing lighting skills, passion, and a great subject. "I love food and I love photography so it was a perfect match!"

Alan has photographed food for several restaurants in the southern California area and has also recently started teaching food photography classes nationally. *Moorish Fusion Cuisine* is Alan's first cookbook project.

**Adriana Hammond, book designer,** majored in industrial design and has a graduate degree in multimedia. She has worked as a graphic designer and 3-D animator for television and advertising at leading companies in Latin America, and coordinated the development of the first multimedia engineering undergraduate program and graduate-level 3-D courses in Colombia. Adriana is an experienced bilingual teacher in design and animation. She is the owner and manager of HUEge Design, a United States–based company that serves local and international clients. She also works as a marketing specialist at one of the biggest investment firms in the United States.

**Tamara L. Kaufman, food stylist,** brings a passion for aesthetics and cooking and seventeen years of culinary experience to her profession as a food stylist. Her career has encompassed positions that include caterer, pastry chef, cooking instructor, food-column writer, and specialty-cheese buyer.

A Bachelor of Arts degree in design from Iowa State University emphasizing psychology and advertising and years of honing her skills have developed her astute sense of three-dimensional design. She has a natural instinct for the arrangement of key elements in a beautiful photographic composition. Tamara balances the natural beauty of food with exceptional attention to detail, without compromising the integrity of the recipe.

She has contributed to hundreds of mouthwatering photos during her freelance career and time at *Reader's Digest* as a staff food stylist.

**Toni Gordillo, assistant chef,** developed a love for cooking at an early age from eating his mother's home cooking in Oaxaca, Mexico. Since he moved to Arizona, he has continually challenged his culinary skills, working in a variety of restaurants and resorts and learning about different cultures and their cuisines. Chef Toni loves experimenting with Mediterranean cuisine, as well as American food with a French twist, putting his special touch on every meal he prepares. When he isn't trying out a new dish, he enjoys watching *fútbol*, exploring the beauty of body ink, and collecting Aztec art.

**Additional thanks and appreciation are owed to**
My friend and mentor Christian G. Chemin, Master Chef of France.
My colleague and friend Hiroaki Kudo, Sushi Master Chef.
My colleague and friend Jose Garces, *Iron Chef America*.
My friend Yoshiki Tsuji, president of Japan's largest cooking school.

IN APPRECIATION OF:

Ali Bendella

Hicham Nafaa

Youssef Sbihi

Adam Zemmouj

Aunt Najia

Mika Nakamura

Patricia Anne Siegert

Cindy Hinton

Kensuke Hosomi

Katsuma Takei

Tatsuo Odani

Yukiko Hirahara

Chika Tokitoh

Randall R. Hammond

Tsuyoshi Hirose

Tevita Takitaki

James Tamasaka

Jared Mateaki

Hari Messer

Keidi Keating

Joe Kapisi

Nalu Akinaka

Elias Akinaka

Published by Emerald Book Company

Austin, TX

www.emeraldbookcompany.com

Distributed by Emerald Book Company

For ordering information or special discounts for bulk purchases, please contact Emerald Book Company at PO Box 91869, Austin, TX  78709, 512.891.6100.


Design and composition by Adriana Hammond and Greenleaf Book Group LLC
Cover design by Adriana Hammond and Greenleaf Book Group LLC
Photography by Alan De Herrera
Food styling by Tamara L. Kaufman


Publisher's Cataloging-In-Publication Data
(Prepared by The Donohue Group, Inc.)
Zairi, Zouhair.
   Moorish fusion cuisine : conquering the New World / Zouhair Zairi. — 1st ed.
     p. : col. ill. ;  cm.
   Includes index.
   ISBN: 978-1-934572-98-6
   1. Cooking, Moroccan.  2. Cooking, North African.  3. Cookbooks.  I. Title.
TX725.N67 Z25 2011
641.592/927/61                                                2011929649

Part of the Tree Neutral® program, which offsets the number of trees consumed in the production and printing of this book by taking proactive steps, such as planting trees in direct proportion to the number of trees used: www.treeneutral.com

Printed in Singapore by Imago
11  12  13  14  15  16    10 9 8 7 6 5 4 3 2 1
First Edition